The Big Fearon Book of Doing Science

Explorations and Adventures in Life, Earth, and Physical Sciences for Grades 1–6

Fearon Teacher Aids
a division of
David S. Lake Publishers
Belmont, California

Illustrator: Bradley Dutsch

ISBN 0-8224-2737-0

Printed in the United States of America

1. 9 8 7 6 5 4 3 2 1

PREFACE

The Big Fearon Book of Doing Science has been specially created to provide you with materials of exceptional educational value in a convenient package. All six of the exciting Doing Science activity books are included in this big book.

Use the table of contents on the next page to find the list of sections in this book. Each section is identified by a handy tab. For a complete list of the activities in any of the six sections, simply use the appropriate tab to turn to that section.

CONTENTS

INTRODUCTION

Teachers greatly influence children's interests. They expose children to new and stimulating topics and help them organize their knowledge. The *Doing Science* series was created to help you encourage children to be curious, to ask questions, to experiment, to learn, and to organize and integrate knowledge. This book will help you teach the processes of science—processes that can be integrated into all parts of our lives.

About This Book

Each **activity page** covers a topic that will easily fit into your science curriculum. The activities help students develop one or more of the following process skills:

- Observing—using the senses to gather information about objects and events.
- Comparing—identifying common and distinguishing characteristics among items or events.
- Measuring—comparatively or quantitatively describing the length, area, volume, mass, or temperature of objects.
- Classifying/Grouping—organizing information into logical categories.
- Sequencing—arranging items or events according to a characteristic.
- Collecting data—collecting and recording information obtained through observation.
- Organizing data—organizing data in a logical way so the results can be interpreted.
- Drawing conclusions—using the skills of inferring, predicting, and/or interpreting.

The **Teacher's Guide** will give you ideas for using each worksheet, including the main science concept, the process emphasis, and the materials list for each activity. The Teacher's Guide pages also include Discovery Questions—questions designed to make your students think and to encourage discussion. These questions are a mixture of specific-answer and open-ended questions that can be used either before, during, or after an activity. So while your students are doing science, they are also learning to think like scientists.

Doing Science

Explorations in Life Science

Process-Oriented Activities for Grades 1–3

PART 1   EXPLORATIONS IN LIFE SCIENCE

CONTENTS

TEACHER'S GUIDE

Animal or Plant?

Purpose

To sort living things into two groups: animals and plants.

Processes

Observing, comparing plants and animals, grouping, recording, and reporting.

Materials

For each student:
- Activity worksheets, pages 22 and 23
- Scissors
- Crayons
- Paste or glue

Procedure

1. Explain that we can divide most living things into two large groups—plants and animals. Ask students the following types of questions:

How are animals different from plants? (Most plants cannot walk or move from where they are planted unless someone moves them. Animals are mobile. Animals have to find their own food to eat or be fed. Plants are able to make their own food.)

How are animals and plants alike? (They are both living things. They grow, change, and adapt to their surroundings, and they are able to reproduce their own kind.)

What are some animals?
What are some plants?

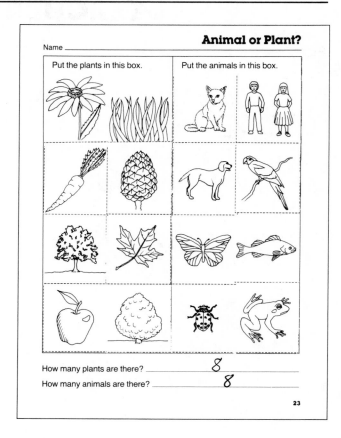

Name _____   **Animal or Plant?**

| Put the plants in this box. | Put the animals in this box. |

How many plants are there? _____ *8*
How many animals are there? _____ *8*

23

2. Have students color and cut out the picture cards on page 22. Then, on page 23, have them sort the cards into two groups—plants and animals. Once all the cards have been sorted, students should paste them on the page and answer the questions.

Discovery Questions

- Are we plants or animals?
- What do all living things have in common?

Incredible Edibles

Purpose

To identify edible parts of plants.

Processes

Observing, comparing edible plant parts, classifying, and recording.

Materials

For each student:
- Activity worksheet, page 24
- Crayons

For the class:
- Variety of edible roots, leaves, and fruits
  Examples:
      Roots—carrots, turnips, radishes
      Leaves—lettuce, spinach
      Fruits—apples, cherries, pumpkins

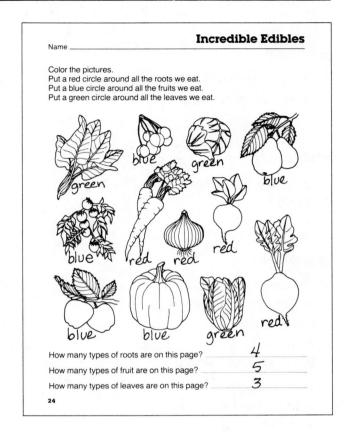

Procedure

1. Show students the plants. Ask them to tell how the plants are all alike (they are all edible). Explain that edible plants can be grouped by certain characteristics. We eat the roots of some plants, the fruits of some plants, and the leaves of some plants. Ask students to tell you which of the plants you have shown them are roots, which are leaves, and which are fruits.

2. Have students put a red circle around all the roots on the worksheet, a blue circle around all the fruits, and a green circle around all the leaves. When they are finished they should answer the questions at the bottom of the page.

Discovery Questions

- Are there any other parts of a plant that we eat?
- Which type of edible part do you like to eat the most?
- Which type of edible part do you like to eat the least?

Make a Plant Grow!

Purpose

To show the development of a plant using properly sequenced pictures.

Processes

Observing, comparing details, and sequencing.

Materials

For each student:
- Activity worksheet, page 25
- Scissors
- Stapler
- Crayons (optional)

For the class:
- Lima beans
- Paper towel
- Water
- Clear plastic bag

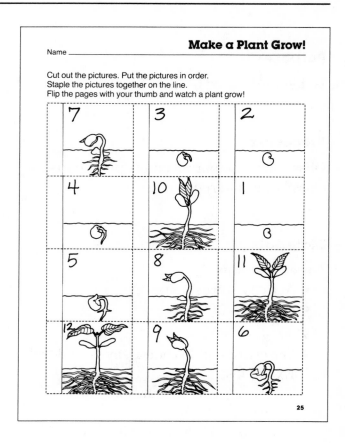

Name _____

Make a Plant Grow!

Cut out the pictures. Put the pictures in order.
Staple the pictures together on the line.
Flip the pages with your thumb and watch a plant grow!

25

Procedure

1. Moisten a folded paper towel. Place several beans on the towel and then place the towel inside the plastic bag. Let the seeds stay on the moist towel for a day or two. Have students observe the growth pattern. Ask them which part of the seed grew first.

2. Explain that when a seed begins to germinate it develops roots, stems, and leaves. Discuss the order in which these steps occur.

3. Duplicate the worksheet on heavy paper. Have students cut out the pictures on the worksheet. Then have students arrange the pictures to show a plant developing from a seed. The picture of the seed should be on top of the pile and the picture of the full-grown plant should be on the bottom of the pile. Once students have sequenced their pictures, they should staple the pages together to form a booklet. By holding the stapled ends of the flip book in one hand and flipping the pages of the book with the other, the pictures will create a "movie." Students may color the pictures if they wish.

Discovery Questions

- What develops after the roots?
- In which direction do the roots grow?
- Do all seeds grow? Why or why not?

Chart-a-Seed

Purpose

To group seeds by color.

Processes

Observing, comparing color, grouping, and reporting.

Materials

For each student:
- Activity worksheet, page 26
- A handful of red, yellow, green, and brown seeds mixed together. (There should be more than one type of seed in at least one of the colors.)
  Examples: red—kidney beans
  yellow—corn, yellow split peas
  green—lima beans, green split peas
  brown—lentils, shelled peanuts
- Paste or glue

Procedure

1. Explain that we can put things that are alike into groups. When we do this, we can observe them more closely and make comparisons more easily. One way to organize items is to make a chart.

2. Have students sort the seeds by color. Then have them place each seed on a square in the correct color row on the chart. When they have done this with all their seeds, ask them to paste each seed to its square. When

their charts are finished they should answer the questions at the bottom of the page.

Discovery Questions:

- Are all the seeds that are the same color the same type?
- How many different types of seed are the same color?
- What is another way we could have grouped the seeds?
- Which color do you think is the most common in nature?

Name _____

Chart-a-Seed

Look at all your seeds.
Sort your seeds into piles of the same color.
Put each seed in a box that names its color.
Paste the seeds down.

red	red	red	red	red	red	red	red	red
yellow	yellow	yellow	yellow	yellow	yellow	yellow	yellow	yellow
green	green	green	green	green	green	green	green	green
brown	brown	brown	brown	brown	brown	brown	brown	brown

Which color has the most seeds? _Answers will vary._
How many seeds does it have? _Answers will vary._
Which color has the fewest seeds? _Answers will vary._
How many seeds does it have? _Answers will vary._

26

Graph-a-Seed

Purpose

To group seeds by shape, and to make and use a graph.

Processes

Observing, comparing shapes, classifying, recording, and reporting.

Materials

For each student:
- Activity worksheet, page 27
- Crayons

Procedure

1. Explain that objects have different shapes. Sometimes it is useful to group objects by their shapes. Ask students to describe different shapes that seeds have.

2. Have students color all the seeds on the worksheet with the suggested colors. Then have them complete the graph and answer the questions at the bottom of the page.

Discovery Questions

- Is there another way we could have grouped these seeds?
- Why do you think seeds have different shapes?
- How might the shape of the seed help it survive?

Finding Leaf Lengths

Purpose

To compare the lengths of leaves.

Processes

Observing, comparing lengths, collecting data, and graphing.

Materials

For each student:

- Activity worksheet, page 28
- Centimeter ruler
- Crayons

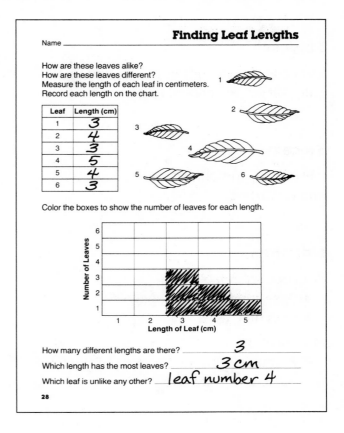

Procedure

1. Explain that a group of things that look alike may not all be exactly the same size. One way the size of such things may differ is in length.

2. Have students measure the lengths of the leaves on the worksheet. Then have them record the lengths on the chart next to the leaves. After they have found the lengths of all the leaves, they should complete the graph. When this is done they should answer the questions at the bottom of the page.

Discovery Questions

- What are other ways we could find differences in size?
- What is the largest leaf you have ever seen?

The Taste Test

Purpose

To recognize the different types of taste—salty, bitter, sweet, and sour.

Processes

Observing, comparing tastes, classifying, and recording.

Materials

For each student:
- Activity worksheet, page 29
- Crayons

For the class:
- Samples of foods for each of the four basic types of taste

Procedure

1. Give each student a small piece of each food sample. Ask them to describe the taste. You might ask them if the taste is mostly salty, mostly bitter, mostly sweet, or mostly sour.

2. On the chalkboard draw a picture that shows the taste receptors on the tongue. It should look something like this:

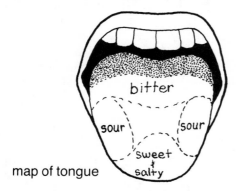

map of tongue

Explain that tongues have taste buds for tasting bitter, sour, sweet, and salty things.

Point out where these taste buds are. You might also discuss how important it is to smell foods when we eat them, since smell enhances the taste of food.

3. Have students color the pictures on the worksheet. Then have them put a red circle around those foods that are bitter, a yellow circle around those that are sweet, a green circle around those that are salty, and a blue circle around those that are sour. If students feel that a particular food has more than one taste, they should put two circles around the item.

Discovery Questions

- Which of the four basic tastes do you like the best?
- How do foods taste different when you have a cold?

Touch and Tell

Purpose

To describe parts of plants by their textures.

Processes

Observing, comparing textures, collecting data, recording, and reporting.

Materials

For each student:
- Activity worksheets, pages 30 and 31
- Four plant parts of different textures
  Examples: tree bark
              thistles
              flowers
              acorns
              twigs
              pine needles
              oak leaves
              sunflower seeds
- Scissors
- Paste or glue

Procedure

1. Explain that our fingers are very sensitive to touch. Our sense of touch helps us gather information about objects. Tell students that we have a lot of different words to describe what we can feel. Ask students to name different textures, and discuss the textures listed on page 31.

2. Have students glue the four items you have given them next to the letters on page 30 and write the name below each item. Then have them cut out the description cards on page 31. Tell them to close their eyes and feel the first object. Ask them to

Name _____

Touch and Tell

Cut out the texture cards on this page.
Use your cards on page 30.

soft · hard · bumpy · smooth · prickly · silky · fluffy · waxy

31

choose the four description cards that best describe the texture of the object. They should then glue these cards in the boxes provided on page 30. Repeat the process for the remaining objects.

Discovery Questions

- How does our sense of touch help us?
- How might textures help protect a plant?

A-Mazing Odors

Purpose

To observe and identify scents.

Processes

Observing, comparing scents, collecting data, recording, and inferring.

Materials

For each student:
- Activity worksheet, page 32
- Crayons
- One cotton ball

For the class or each group of students:
- Sixteen sticks or pencils
- Sixteen cotton balls
- Sixteen 2″ × 4″ art paper flags—3 red, 3 yellow, 2 purple, 2 orange, 3 blue, 3 green
- Two different liquid scents
  Examples: onion extract
  flower cologne
  almond extract
  mint extract
  vanilla extract
  lemon extract
- Modeling clay
- Tape

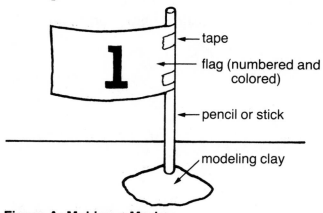

Figure A: Making a Marker

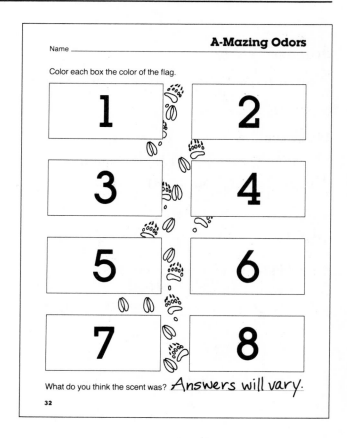

Procedure

1. Before class make two sets of flags. Write numbers on them as follows:

Flag Set 1	Flag Set 2
#1 red	#1 yellow
#2 blue	#2 green
#3 green	#3 blue
#4 purple	#4 orange
#5 yellow	#5 red
#6 orange	#6 purple
#7 red	#7 yellow
#8 blue	#8 green

Construct markers with the flags by taping the flags to the sticks or pencils. (See Figure A.) Randomly place the markers throughout the room, mixing markers from sets 1 and 2 together. Use the clay to hold up the markers on the floor or tables.

2. Dampen eight cotton balls with one of the scents. Place the cotton at the base of each marker in set #1. Repeat for the markers in set #2, using the second scent.

3. Give each student a worksheet, crayons, and a cotton ball dampened with the second scent. Ask students to "track" the scent by finding all the markers that have the same scent as their cotton ball. As they find each marker, ask them to color the flags on the worksheet the same color as the flag on the marker. They may "track" the numbers in any order they wish. When they are finished, ask them to write down what they think the scent was.

Discovery Questions

- In what ways is our sense of smell important to us?
- In what ways is smell important to other animals?

How Frogs Grow

Purpose

To describe the life cycle of a frog by properly sequencing pictures.

Processes

Observing, comparing development stages, sequencing, and recording.

Materials

For each student:
- Activity worksheets, pages 33 and 34
- Shoe-box top or a paper plate with a lip
- Five pieces 1″ × 1″ corrugated cardboard or sponge
- Scissors
- Crayons
- Paste or glue

Procedure

1. Discuss the life cycle of a frog. The sequence can be visually displayed using the pictures on page 33.

2. Have students color and cut out the pictures on pages 33 and 34. Then have them paste the cardboard or sponge to the back of the five life-cycle pictures. After they have finished this, tell them to make a scene on the shoe-box top or plate using all the pictures. Students should glue the pieces down when their scene is finished. Then they should draw an arrow from one life-cycle picture to the next so that the arrows show the sequence of frog development.

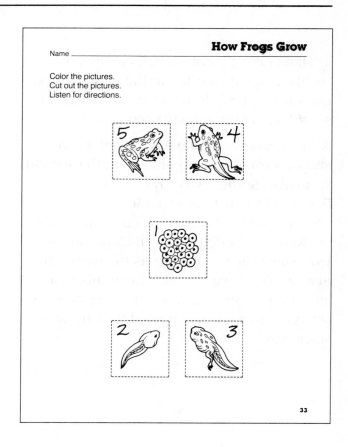

Discovery Questions

- How long does it take for a human to become full-grown?
- How long does it take for a human to become full-grown?
- Why does it take longer for some things to grow up than others?

Hop, Skip, and Jump

Purpose

To recognize that there are different ways in which animals move.

Processes

Observing body parts, comparing, classifying, and recording.

Materials

For each student:
- Activity worksheet, page 35
- Crayons (optional)

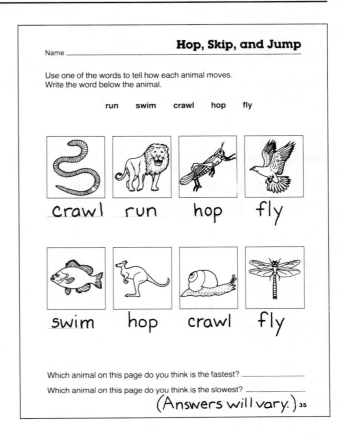

Procedure

1. Discuss the various ways in which animals can move—walking, running, crawling, hopping, and flying. Explain that while some animals, such as humans, can move in more than one way, they usually have a primary form of motion.

2. Have students write the primary form of motion below each animal shown on the worksheet. They may color the pictures if they wish.

Discovery Questions

- What are the different ways that humans can move?
- What are some animals that move faster than humans?
- What are some animals that move slower than humans?

Feathers and Fur

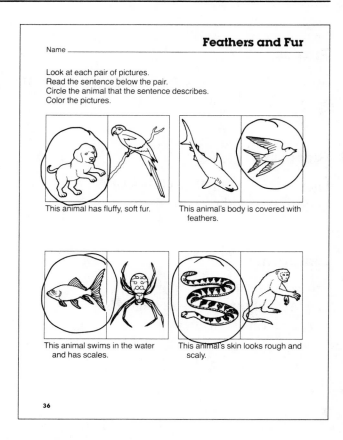

Purpose

To identify what type of body covering particular animals have.

Processes

Observing, comparing body coverings, classifying, and recording.

Materials

For each student:
- Activity worksheet, page 36
- Crayons

Name _____   **Feathers and Fur**

Look at each pair of pictures.
Read the sentence below the pair.
Circle the animal that the sentence describes.
Color the pictures.

This animal has fluffy, soft fur.   This animal's body is covered with feathers.

This animal swims in the water and has scales.   This animal's skin looks rough and scaly.

36

Procedure

1. Ask students to tell you what covers a cat's body, what covers a bird's body, what covers a snake's body, what covers a fish's body, and what covers a frog's body. Discuss their answers and the textures of the skin coverings.

2. Tell students to look at the pairs of pictures on the worksheet and to circle the picture in each pair that is described by the sentence below the pair. When they are finished, have them color the pictures.

Discovery Questions

- What covers our body?
- What texture is our skin?
- Is there any other kind of animal that has the same texture of skin as ours?

Where Do They Live?

Purpose

To compare and group land and water animals.

Processes

Observing, comparing, grouping, and recording.

Materials

For each student:
- Activity worksheets, pages 37, 38, and 39
- Scissors
- Crayons
- Paste or glue

For the class:
- Pictures of the ocean and of the forest (*National Geographic* is a good source for these types of pictures.)

Procedure

1. Show students the pictures. Ask them to tell you what they represent. Explain that the pictures show two types of places where animals can live. Ask students to name some animals that could live in the ocean scene and in the forest scene. Discuss the characteristics that distinguish ocean animals from land animals. For example, fish have streamlined bodies and fins that help them swim easily and quickly, but their bodies would not help them move on land. Deer have legs that let them move on land, but they don't have gills which would let them breathe in the water.

Where Do They Live?

Name _____

Put the animals that live on the land in the picture below. Paste the cards to make a scene.

38

2. Have students color and cut out the picture cards on page 37. Then have them match each animal to its proper environment on page 38 or page 39. When they have grouped all the cards, have them paste the cards down to create a scene.

Discovery Questions

- How could you tell if an animal lives on the land or in the water?
- Are there animals that live both in the water and on the land?
- What characteristics do land animals have that prevent them from living in the water?
- What characteristics do water animals have that prevent them from living on the land?

Parts That Protect

Purpose

To identify body parts that protect animals from enemies.

Processes

Observing, comparing body parts, identifying, and recording.

Materials

For each student:
- Activity worksheet, page 40
- Crayons

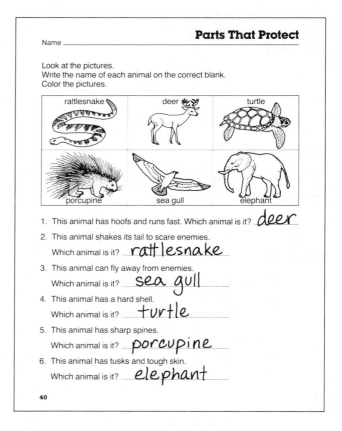

Procedure

1. Ask students if they know ways in which an animal can protect itself. Explain that many animals have a special body part to help protect them from enemies. Discuss the various types of body parts used for protection—claws, armor or shells, teeth, odor, horns, tough skin, and so on.

2. Have children write the answers to the questions in the blanks on the worksheet. They should then color the pictures.

Discovery Questions

- How can we protect ourselves from enemies?
- How do horns help some animals protect themselves?
- How do ears help some animals protect themselves?
- How do feet help some animals protect themselves?

Food Chain Mobile

Purpose

To create a mobile that shows the sequence of a food chain.

Processes

Observing, comparing, sequencing, and recording.

Materials

For each student:
- Activity worksheets, pages 41 and 42
- 20″ colored string or yarn
- Scissors
- Crayons
- Paste or glue

Procedure

1. Ask students if they know what a food chain is. Explain that a food chain consists of a series of animals that eat plants and other animals. Tell them that an animal that eats plants is called a primary consumer. A grasshopper would be called a primary consumer because it eats grass. A primary consumer is at the bottom of the food chain. Ask students to think of other primary consumers (note: all plant eaters are primary consumers). Continue by telling students that animals who eat primary consumers are called secondary consumers. A secondary consumer would be the next animal in the food chain. A frog would be a secondary consumer because it eats grasshoppers. If a snake eats the frog, then the snake would be the third consumer in the food chain. And if a hawk eats the snake,

Name _____

Food Chain Mobile

Color the animals.
Write the name of each animal in the blank next to the animal.
Cut out the pictures.
Put the pictures in order to make a food chain.
Listen for directions on how to make a mobile.

4   grasshopper

2   snake

41

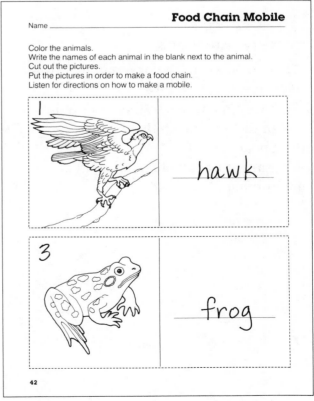

Name _____

Food Chain Mobile

Color the animals.
Write the names of each animal in the blank next to the animal.
Cut out the pictures.
Put the pictures in order to make a food chain.
Listen for directions on how to make a mobile.

1   hawk

3   frog

42

the hawk would be the fourth animal in the chain. Since the hawk has no natural enemies, it would also be the final animal in the chain.

2. Duplicate the worksheets on heavy paper. Have students write the name of each animal in the blank next to the animal's picture. Then have them color and cut out the cards. They should arrange the pictures on their desks with the fourth consumer (hawk) at the top of the desk and the primary consumer (grasshopper) at the bottom of the desk. Have them fold the cards in half (with the picture facing out) and glue the two sides together, making sure that the string is between them. (See Figure A.) They should put the picture of the fourth consumer at the top of the string and work their way down. They can then hang the mobile by its string.

Discovery Questions

- What are some of the other animals that make up a food chain?
- What would happen to the other animals if one of the animals in the chain disappeared?
- What might a food chain be in an ocean environment? a forest? a desert?

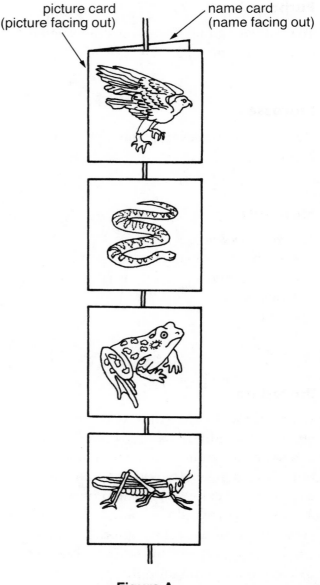

Figure A

Animal Circles

Purpose

To use Venn diagrams to classify animals by number of legs and by habitat.

Processes

Observing, comparing number of legs and habitats, and grouping.

Materials

For each student:
- Activity worksheets, pages 43 and 44
- Scissors
- Crayons
- Four pieces 24" yarn; three yellow and one red

Procedure

1. Duplicate the activity pages on heavy paper. Have students cut out the animal cards on page 43 and the label cards on page 44. Ask students to color the labels red or yellow as indicated on page 44. Next, have students tie the yarn into loops, so they each have three yellow loops and one red loop.

2. Ask students to put their red loops on their desks. Tell them to make the loop into the shape of a circle and put the red label ANIMALS FOUND ON LAND inside the circle. Then have them overlap the red circle with the three yellow circles so the circles look like Figure A.

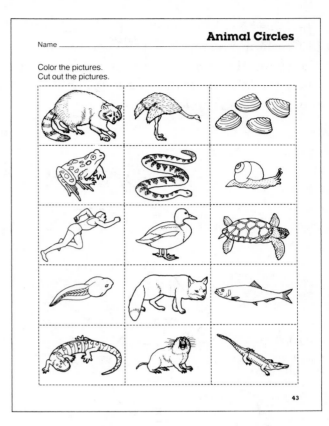

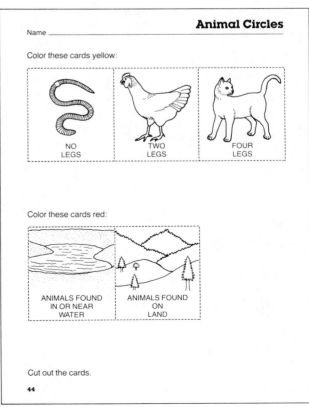

The labels NO LEGS, TWO LEGS, and FOUR LEGS should be placed in the yellow circles. Make sure the students put the yellow labels *outside* of the areas of intersection between the yellow and red loops.

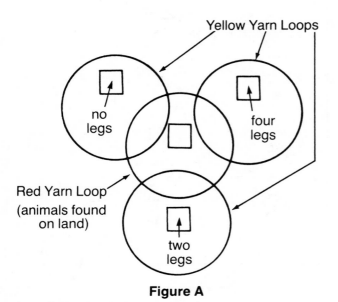

Figure A

3. Point out to students that the spaces where the red loop and the yellow loops overlap are called *intersections*. Tell them that these intersections are the places to put things that belong in both the red loop and one of the yellow loops. Have students group the animal cards by number of legs. Then have them put the cards in the appropriate yellow circles. Ask students to find the animals in each yellow circle that live on land. Tell them to move those animals into the intersection spaces. When they have finished the exercise, you might ask students to explain why we would want to organize the cards this way.

4. Repeat the exercise using the label ANIMALS FOUND IN OR NEAR WATER instead of the label ANIMALS FOUND ON LAND.

Discovery Questions

- What are some other animals we could put in these categories?
- What are some other characteristics we could use to group animals?

ACTIVITY WORKSHEETS

Name _____

Color all the pictures.
Cut out the pictures.
Use your picture cards on page 23.

Explorations in Life Science, © 1987 David S. Lake Publishers

Name _____

Put the plants in this box.	Put the animals in this box.

How many plants are there? _____

How many animals are there? _____

Incredible Edibles

Color the pictures.
Put a red circle around all the roots we eat.
Put a blue circle around all the fruits we eat.
Put a green circle around all the leaves we eat.

How many types of roots are on this page? _____

How many types of fruit are on this page? _____

How many types of leaves are on this page? _____

Make a Plant Grow!

Name _____

Cut out the pictures. Put the pictures in order.
Staple the pictures together on the line.
Flip the pages with your thumb and watch a plant grow!

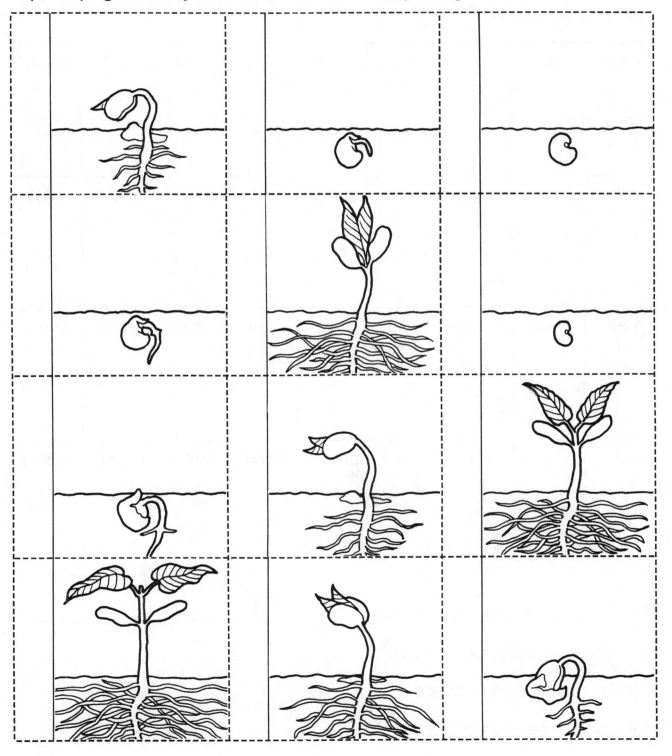

Chart-a-Seed

Look at all your seeds.
Sort your seeds into piles of the same color.
Put each seed in a box that names its color.
Paste the seeds down.

red	red	red	red	red	red	red	red	red
yellow	yellow	yellow	yellow	yellow	yellow	yellow	yellow	yellow
green	green	green	green	green	green	green	green	green
brown	brown	brown	brown	brown	brown	brown	brown	brown

Which color has the most seeds? _____

How many seeds does it have? _____

Which color has the fewest seeds? _____

How many seeds does it have? _____

Explorations in Life Science, © 1987 David S. Lake Publishers

Graph-a-Seed

Name _____

Color all the seeds like this

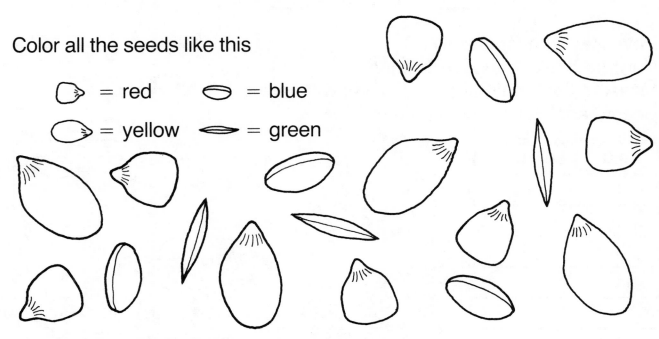

    = red   = blue

    = yellow   = green

Count all the seeds that are the same color.
Make a graph. For each seed shape, color the number of boxes that
   tells how many.

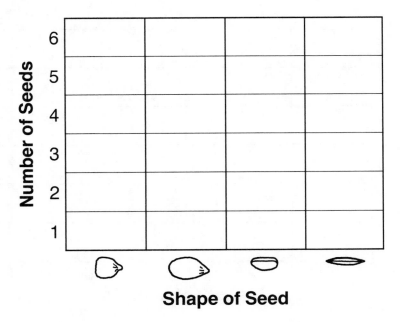

Shape of Seed

Circle the shape that has the greatest number of seeds:

Circle the shape that has the greatest number of seeds:

Circle the shape that has the greatest number of seeds:

Finding Leaf Lengths

Name _____

How are these leaves alike?
How are these leaves different?
Measure the length of each leaf in centimeters.
Record each length on the chart.

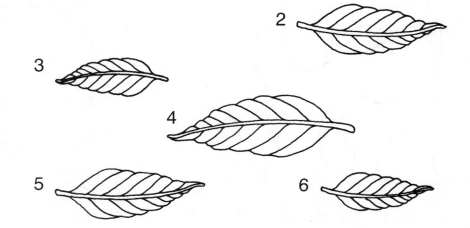

Leaf	Length (cm)
1	
2	
3	
4	
5	
6	

Color the boxes to show the number of leaves for each length.

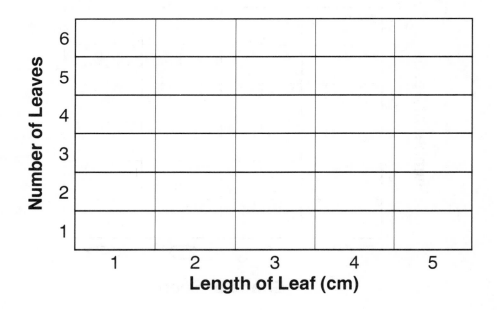

How many different lengths are there? _____

Which length has the most leaves? _____

Which leaf is unlike any other? _____

Explorations in Life Science, © 1987 David S. Lake Publishers

Name _____

Color the pictures.
Put a red circle around all the things that taste bitter.
Put a yellow circle around all the things that taste sweet.
Put a green circle around all the things that taste salty.
Put a blue circle around all the things that taste sour.
If something has two types of taste, put two circles around it.

Name _____

Paste each item next to a letter.
Write its name.

A.   B.   C.   D.

_____   _____   _____   _____

Look at your texture cards.
Pick four cards that best describe how each item feels.
Paste the cards in the boxes below.

Item A	Item B	Item C	Item D

Name _____

Cut out the texture cards on this page.
Use your cards on page 30.

soft	soft	soft	soft
hard	hard	hard	hard
bumpy	bumpy	bumpy	bumpy
smooth	smooth	smooth	smooth
prickly	prickly	prickly	prickly
silky	silky	silky	silky
fluffy	fluffy	fluffy	fluffy
waxy	waxy	waxy	waxy

Name _____

Color each box the color of the flag.

1	2
3	4
5	6
7	8

What do you think the scent was? _____

Name _____

Color the pictures.
Cut out the pictures.
Listen for directions.

Name _____

Color the pictures.
Cut out the pictures.
Listen for directions.

Hop, Skip, and Jump

Use one of the words to tell how each animal moves.
Write the word below the animal.

run   swim   crawl   hop   fly

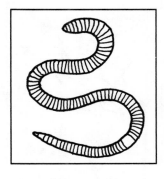      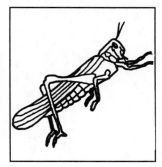   

_____   _____   _____   _____

_____   _____   _____   _____

Which animal on this page do you think is the fastest? _____

Which animal on this page do you think is the slowest? _____

Name _____

Look at each pair of pictures.
Read the sentence below the pair.
Circle the animal that the sentence describes.
Color the pictures.

This animal has fluffy, soft fur.

This animal's body is covered with feathers.

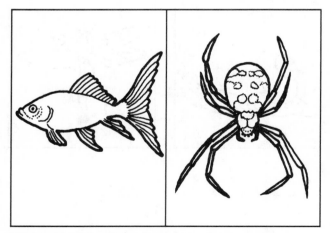

This animal swims in the water and has scales.

This animal's skin looks rough and scaly.

Explorations in Life Science, © 1987 David S. Lake Publishers

Where Do They Live?

Color the animals.
Cut out the animals.
Use your cards on pages 38 and 39.

Explorations in Life Science, © 1987 David S. Lake Publishers

Where Do They Live?

Name _____

Put the animals that live on the land in the picture below.
Paste the cards to make a scene.

Where Do They Live?

Put the animals that live in the ocean in the picture below.
Paste the cards to make a scene.

Parts That Protect

Name _____

Look at the pictures.
Write the name of each animal on the correct blank.
Color the pictures.

rattlesnake   deer   turtle

porcupine   sea gull   elephant

1. This animal has hoofs and runs fast. Which animal is it? _____

2. This animal shakes its tail to scare enemies.

   Which animal is it? _____

3. This animal can fly away from enemies.

   Which animal is it? _____

4. This animal has a hard shell.

   Which animal is it? _____

5. This animal has sharp spines.

   Which animal is it? _____

6. This animal has tusks and tough skin.

   Which animal is it? _____

Explorations in Life Science, © 1987 David S. Lake Publishers

Name _____

Color the animals.
Write the name of each animal in the blank next to the animal.
Cut out the pictures.
Put the pictures in order to make a food chain.
Listen for directions on how to make a mobile.

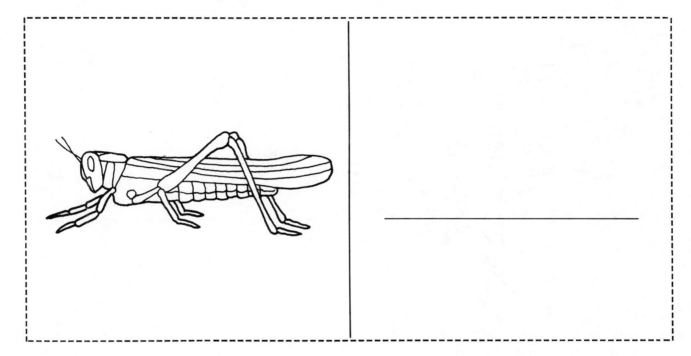

_____

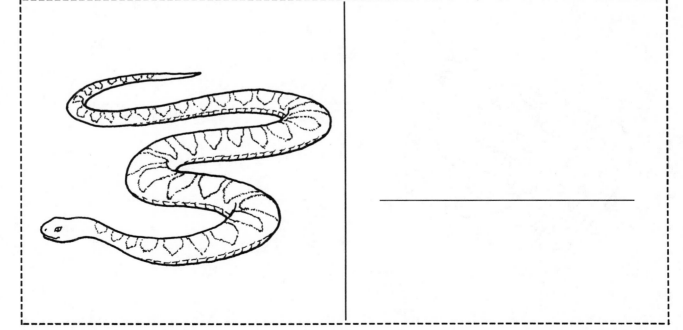

_____

Food Chain Mobile

Color the animals.
Write the names of each animal in the blank next to the animal.
Cut out the pictures.
Put the pictures in order to make a food chain.
Listen for directions on how to make a mobile.

_____

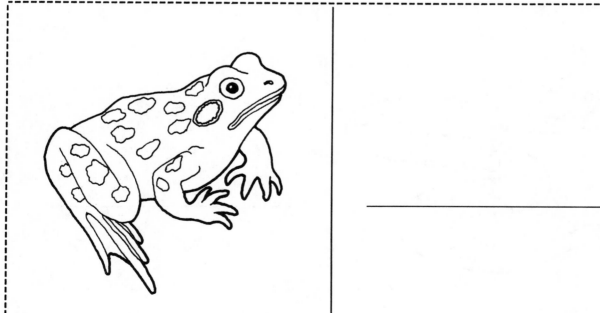

_____

Explorations in Life Science, © 1987 David S. Lake Publishers

Animal Circles

Color the pictures.
Cut out the pictures.

Animal Circles

Color these cards yellow:

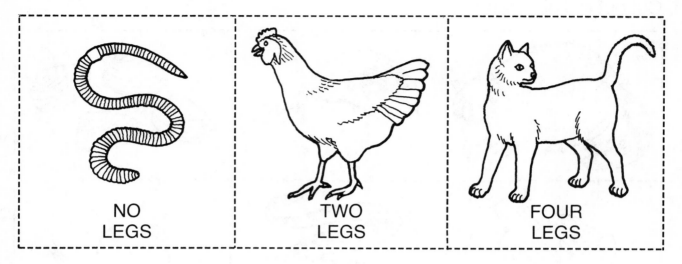

NO
LEGS

TWO
LEGS

FOUR
LEGS

Color these cards red:

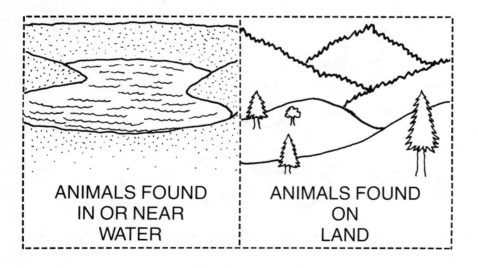

ANIMALS FOUND
IN OR NEAR
WATER

ANIMALS FOUND
ON
LAND

Cut out the cards.

Explorations in *Life Science,* © 1987 David S. Lake Publishers

Doing Science

Explorations in Physical Science

Process-Oriented Activities for Grades 1–3

PART 2   EXPLORATIONS IN PHYSICAL SCIENCE

CONTENTS

TEACHER'S GUIDE

What's the Matter?

Purpose

To classify objects into three groups: solids, liquids, and gases.

Processes

Observing, comparing forms of matter, classifying, recording, and reporting.

Materials

For each student:
- Activity worksheet, page 22
- Crayons (optional)

Procedure

1. Discuss the three states of matter—solid, liquid, and gas—and their properties. Ask students the following types of questions:

What are some solids in this room?

Can we see any liquids in this room?

What are some liquids we use at home?

(Some possible answers might be milk, cleaning fluids, or orange juice.)

Are there any gases present in this room?

Can you think of any gases besides air?

(Some possible answers might be helium in balloons, or bubbles in soda.)

Discuss students' answers.

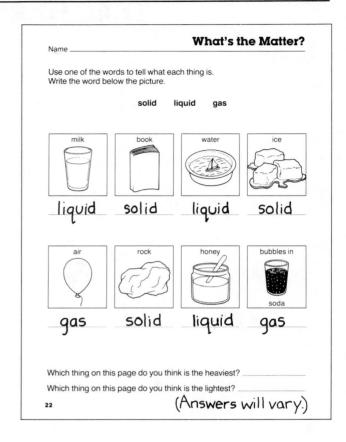

2. Have students write *solid*, *liquid*, or *gas* below each object shown on the worksheet. They may color the pictures if they wish. Then have students answer the questions at the bottom of the worksheet.

Discovery Questions

- What type of matter is a cloud?
- What type of matter is a person?
- What are some things that are combinations of different types of matter?

Touch and Tell

Purpose

To describe solids by their textures.

Processes

Observing, comparing textures, collecting data, recording, and reporting.

Materials

For each student:

- Activity worksheets, pages 23 and 24
- Four small solids of different textures
  Examples: pebble
                 sandpaper
                 burlap
                 tree bark
                 cotton ball
                 seashell
- Scissors
- Paste or glue

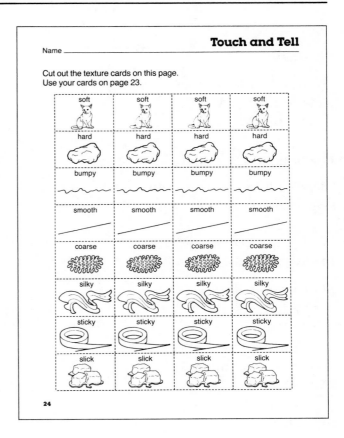

Procedure

1. Explain that our fingers are very sensitive to touch. Our sense of touch helps us gather information about objects. Tell students that we have a lot of different words to describe what we can feel. Ask students to name different textures, and discuss the textures listed on page 24.

2. Have students glue the four items you have given them next to the letters on page 23 and write the name below each item. Then have them cut out the description cards on page 24. Tell them to close their eyes and feel the first object. Ask them to choose the four description cards that best describe the texture of the object. They should then glue these cards in the boxes provided on page 23. Repeat the process for the remaining objects.

Discovery Questions

- How can our sense of touch help us?
- What are some ways you could describe liquids using your sense of touch?

Ice to Steam!

Purpose

To show how a solid can change to a liquid and then to a gas.

Processes

Observing, comparing details, and sequencing.

Materials

For each student:
- Activity worksheet, page 25
- Scissors
- Stapler
- Crayons (optional)

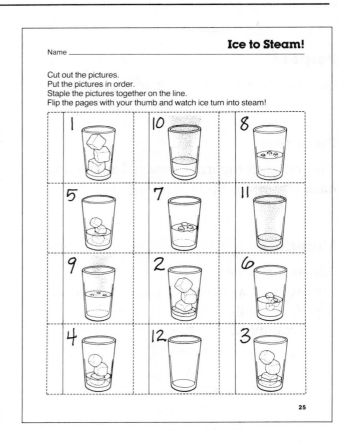

Procedure

1. Discuss what happens when ice is left in the sun and when water is heated. Explain that ice turning to water is an example of a solid changing to a liquid, and water turning to steam is an example of a liquid changing to a gas.

2. Duplicate the worksheet on heavy paper. Have students cut out the pictures on the worksheet. Then have students arrange the pictures to show ice turning to water turning to steam. The picture of the ice should be on top of the pile, and the picture of the empty glass should be on the bottom of the pile. Once students have sequenced their pictures, they should staple the pages together to form a booklet. By holding the stapled ends of the flip book in one hand and flipping the pages of the book with the other, the pictures will create a "movie." Students may color the pictures if they wish.

Discovery Questions

- What happens when you put water into a freezer?
- How could you change a liquid into a solid?
- How could you change a liquid into a gas?

What Does It Attract?

Purpose

To identify objects that a magnet will attract.

Processes

Observing, comparing, grouping, recording, and reporting.

Materials

For each student:
- Activity worksheets, pages 26 and 27
- Crayons
- Scissors
- Paste or glue
- Magnet

Procedure

1. Explain that a magnet is a special piece of metal that can pick up, pull, or stick to some objects. Ask students to guess what items in the classroom might attract magnets. Have them test each object with a magnet.

2. Have students color and cut out the picture cards on page 26. Then, on page 27, have them sort the cards into two groups—things that a magnet will attract and things that a magnet won't attract. (You might want to bring the objects listed on the cards, so students can test them.) Once the cards have been sorted, students should paste them on the page and answer the questions.

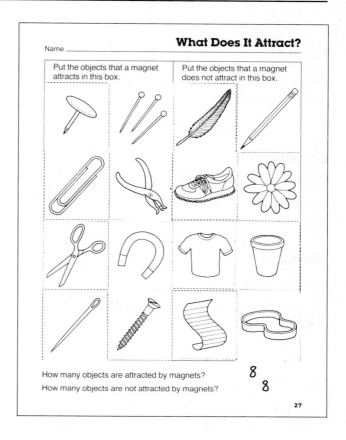

Name _____

What Does It Attract?

Put the objects that a magnet attracts in this box. | Put the objects that a magnet does not attract in this box.

How many objects are attracted by magnets? 8
How many objects are not attracted by magnets? 8

27

Discovery Questions

- Will a magnet attract anything that is made of metal?
- Will magnets of different sizes attract the same things?
- Will magnets of different shapes attract the same things?

Graph-a-Magnet

Purpose

To group magnets by shape, and to make and use a graph.

Processes

Observing, comparing shapes, classifying, recording, and reporting.

Materials

For each student:
- Activity worksheet, page 28
- Crayons

Procedure

1. Explain that magnets have different shapes. Sometimes it is useful to group objects by their shapes. Ask students to describe the different shapes that magnets can have.

2. Have students color all the magnets on the worksheet with the suggested colors. Then have them complete the graph and answer the questions at the bottom of the page.

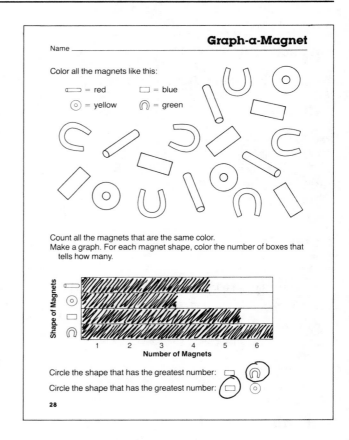

Discovery Questions

- Is there another way we could have grouped these magnets?
- Why do you think we need different shapes of magnets?
- Does the shape of a magnet affect its pull?

North and South

Purpose

To show that like poles repel and unlike poles attract.

Processes

Applying, observing, comparing, and recording.

Materials

For each student:
- Activity worksheet, page 29
- Two bar magnets (with north and south poles marked)

Procedure

1. Discuss the fact that a magnet will sometimes pull another magnet toward it and sometimes push the other magnet away. Explain that when two magnets come together we say they attract, and when two magnets are pushed away from each other we say they repel.

2. Have students place the two north poles together and draw a picture of what happens on the worksheet. Repeat the process putting the two south poles together, and putting a north and south pole together.

3. Explain that some parts of a magnet are stronger than other parts. Tell students that the strongest parts of a magnet are called poles. Every magnet always has two poles—a north pole and a south pole. Show students the poles on the bar magnets.

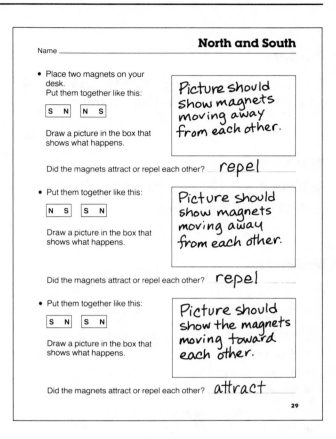

Discovery Questions

- When do the magnets attract each other?
- When do the magnets repel each other?
- Do magnets of other shapes have north and south poles that behave this way?

Charge It!

Purpose

To observe static charge, and to experiment with attracting and repelling charges.

Processes

Applying, observing, comparing, recording, and reporting.

Materials

For each student:
- Activity worksheet, page 30

For each group of five students:
- Two balloons
- Two 12″-long pieces of thread
- Two 12″ × 3″ pieces of nylon (an old nylon stocking works well)
- Piece of wool or fur

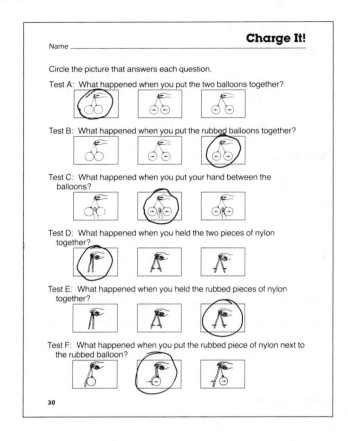

Procedure

1. Before class, blow up the balloons and tie a piece of thread to each. (You may want to blow up a few extra balloons in case any pop.) Divide the class into groups of five. Tell students that for each test they perform, they should observe what happens and record it on their worksheets. Then have the students perform the following tests:

Test A: Have one student hold the two strings together in one hand with his or her arm outstretched. Record what happens. (The balloons hang freely just touching each other.)

Test B: Have a student charge the balloons by rubbing them with the piece of wool or fur. Then a student should hold the balloons in the same manner as in Test A. Record what happens. (The balloons repel each other.)

Test C: Ask a student to place a hand between the two charged balloons. Record what happens. (The charged balloons touch the child's hand because it is electrically neutral.)

Test D: Have a student hold the pieces of nylon together at one end. Record what happens. (The nylon pieces hang freely.)

Test E: Have a student charge the nylon pieces by putting the pieces on a piece of paper and rubbing them quickly with his or her hand. Someone should then hold the pieces of nylon together at one end. Record what happens. (The nylon pieces repel each other.)

Test F: Have a student bring a piece of charged nylon next to a charged balloon. Record what happens. (The nylon attracts the balloon.)

2. You might explain to students that an electrical charge is a quantity of energy that can be given to an object. Some objects, such as balloons and nylon pieces, become electrically charged when you rub them. You might also discuss the two types of charge—positive and negative—and how objects can gain or lose charge.

Discovery Questions

- How are electrically charged objects like magnets?
- What are some other objects that demonstrate static electricity?

Energy Circles

Purpose

To use Venn diagrams to classify objects by the type of energy they produce.

Processes

Observing, comparing energy forms, and grouping.

Materials

For each student:
- Activity worksheets, pages 31 and 32
- Scissors
- Crayons
- Four pieces of 24″ yarn; three yellow and one red.

Procedure

1. Demonstrate sound energy, light energy, and mechanical energy.

2. Duplicate the activity pages on heavy paper. Have students cut out the object cards on page 31 and the label cards on page 32. Ask students to color the labels red or yellow as indicated on page 32. Next, have students tie the yarn into loops, so they each have three yellow loops and one red loop.

3. Ask students to put their red loops on their desks. Tell them to make the loop into the shape of a circle, and put the red label THINGS THAT USE ELECTRICITY inside the circle. Then have them overlap the red circle with the three yellow circles so the circles look like Figure A.

Name _____   **Energy Circles**

Color the pictures.
Cut out the pictures.

31

Name _____   **Energy Circles**

Color these cards yellow:

| SOUND ENERGY | LIGHT ENERGY | MECHANICAL ENERGY |

Color these cards red:

| THINGS THAT USE ELECTRICITY | THINGS THAT DON'T USE ELECTRICITY |

Cut out the cards.
32

The labels LIGHT ENERGY, SOUND ENERGY, and MECHANICAL ENERGY should be placed in the yellow circles. Make sure the students put the yellow labels *outside* the areas of intersection between the yellow and red loops.

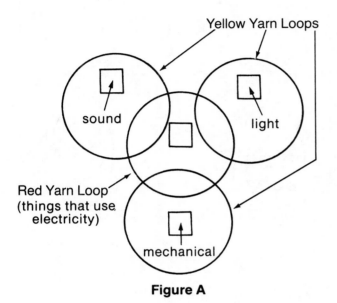

Figure A

4. Point out to students that the spaces where the red loop and the yellow loops overlap are called *intersections*. Tell them that these intersections are the places to put things that belong in both the red loop and one of the yellow loops. Have students group the object cards by the type of energy the objects produce. Then have them put the cards in the appropriate yellow circles. Ask students to find the objects in each yellow circle that use electricity. Tell them to move those objects into the intersection spaces. When they have finished the exercise, you might ask students to explain why we would want to organize the cards this way.

5. Repeat the exercise using the label THINGS THAT DON'T USE ELECTRICITY instead of the label THINGS THAT USE ELECTRICITY.

Discovery Questions

- What are some other objects we could put in these categories?
- Can you think of anything that produces all three types of energy?

What Gives Us Light?

Purpose

To identify different sources of light.

Processes

Observing, comparing, classifying, and recording.

Materials

For each student:
- Activity worksheet, page 33
- Crayons

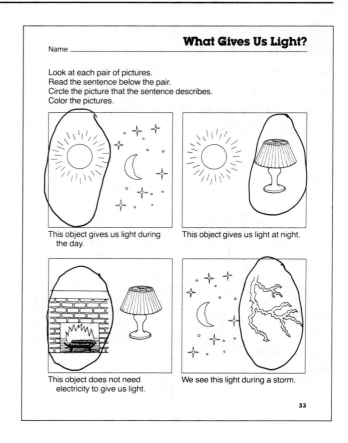

What Gives Us Light?

Name _____

Look at each pair of pictures.
Read the sentence below the pair.
Circle the picture that the sentence describes.
Color the pictures.

This object gives us light during the day.

This object gives us light at night.

This object does not need electricity to give us light.

We see this light during a storm.

33

Procedure

1. Explain to students that many things give off light. Ask students to identify what is giving off light in the classroom. Discuss their answers. You might also explain the concepts of natural and artificial light.

2. Tell students to look at the pairs of pictures on the worksheet. Have them circle the picture in each pair that is described by the sentence below the pair. When they are finished have them color the pictures.

Discovery Questions

- Does fire give off natural or artificial light?
- What animals make their own light?
- Do all things that give off light also give off heat?

Does Light Go Through?

Purpose

To classify objects by opacity.

Processes

Inferring, applying, observing, collecting data, comparing, and recording.

Materials

For each student:
- Activity worksheet, page 34

For the class:
- Flashlight
- Paper towel
- Heavy cardboard
- Foil
- Black construction paper
- Plastic wrap
- Glass
- Wax paper
- Wood

Procedure

1. Show students the various materials. For each item ask them if they think a lot of light, a little light, or no light will go through it. Have students mark their guesses on their worksheets. Then turn off the lights and darken the room. Hold each object in front of the flashlight so students can check their guesses. Turn the lights back on and have students complete the worksheet.

2. Explain to students that we group items by the amount of light they let through. Tell students that objects that allow a great deal of light to pass through them are called *transparent*; objects that don't let any light through them are called *opaque*; and objects that let some light through them are called *translucent*. Then ask students to answer the questions at the bottom of the worksheet.

Discovery Questions

- Can you see through one piece of paper? How about five?
- What changes when you add more sheets of paper?
- What do you see if you hold your hand behind a piece of wax paper?

Does Light Go Through?

Name _____

Think about each item on this page.
Do you think a flashlight can shine through it?
If you think a lot of light would shine through it, leave the first box blank like this: ☐
If you think a little light would shine through it, color the first box like this: ▨
If you think no light would shine through it, color the first box like this: ▓
When your teacher tests each item, mark what you see in the second box.

	Guess	Actual		Guess	Actual
Paper Towel		▨	Plastic Wrap		
Cardboard		▓	Glass		
Aluminum Foil		▓	Wax Paper		▨
Black Paper		▓	Wood		▓

Which things are opaque? cardboard, foil, black paper & wood
Which things are transparent? glass and plastic wrap
Which things are translucent? paper towel and wax paper

34

Finding Shadow Lengths

Purpose

To compare the lengths of shadows.

Processes

Observing, comparing lengths, collecting data, and graphing.

Materials

For each student:
- Activity worksheet, page 35
- Centimeter ruler
- Crayons

Procedure

1. Explain that a group of objects that look alike may not all be exactly the same size. One way the size of such objects may differ is in length.

2. Have students measure the lengths of the shadows on the worksheet. (Make sure they do not include the rock that the shadow is coming from.) Then have them record the lengths on the chart next to the shadows. After they have found the lengths of all the shadows, they should complete the graph. When this is done they should answer the questions at the bottom of the page.

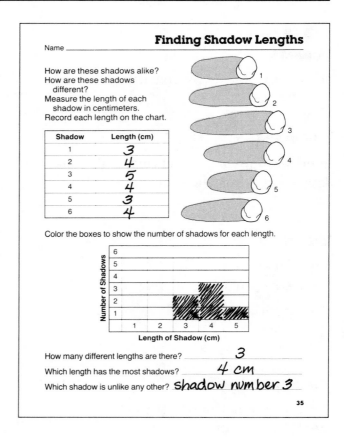

Discovery Questions

- What are other ways we could find difference in size?
- What makes the shadows change size?
- When do you see the longest shadows?

City Noises/Country Noises

Purpose

To compare and group objects that make noise in the country and in the city.

Processes

Observing, comparing, grouping, and recording.

Materials

For each student:
- Activity worksheets, pages 36, 37, and 38
- Scissors
- Crayons
- Paste or glue

For the class:
- Pictures of the country and of the city

Procedure

1. Show the students the pictures. Ask them to tell you what they represent. Explain that the pictures show two types of places where you can hear different things. Ask students to tell you some of the noises you might hear in each place.

2. Have students color and cut out the picture cards on page 36. Then have them match each object to the place where you

might hear it on page 37 or 38. When they have grouped all the cards, have them paste the cards down to create a scene.

Discovery Questions

- What are some sounds you might hear on a beach?
- What are some sounds you might hear in a forest?
- What are some sounds you might hear at home?

Now Hear This!

Purpose

To identify sounds that we can and cannot hear.

Processes

Observing, comparing, classifying, and recording.

Materials

- Activity worksheet, page 39
- Crayons

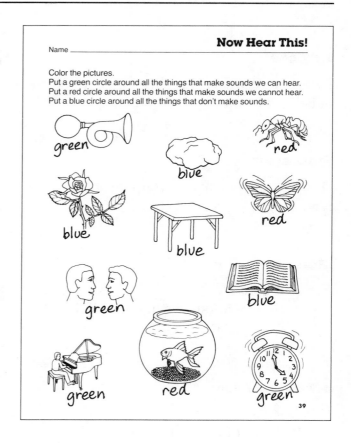

Procedure

1. Discuss the concept of sound vibration. Explain that there are things which vibrate and make sounds which are too high or low for us to hear. There are also some sounds that are not too high or low but are simply not loud enough for us to hear. You should also discuss things that do not vibrate, and therefore do not make sounds.

2. Have students color the pictures on the worksheet. Then have them put a green circle around all the objects that make sounds we can hear, a red circle around the objects that make sounds we cannot hear, and a blue circle around the objects that do not make sounds.

Discovery Questions

- What are some ways to make sounds with a rubber band?
- How do we know that some things make sounds if we can't hear them?
- What do all the things that don't make sound have in common?

Moving Machines

Purpose

To identify machines that can help us do work.

Processes

Observing, comparing, classifying, and recording.

Materials

For each student:
- Activity worksheet, page 40
- Crayons

Moving Machines

Name _____

Sandy wants to move a box.
It is too heavy to lift.
Find all the objects in the pictures that could help Sandy move the box.
Put a red circle around the objects that would pull the box.
Put a blue circle around the objects that would push the box.

Are all the objects with circles around them machines? (yes) no

Look at the objects that are not circled. Which ones are machines?
scissors, hammer, and fishing pole

Which object would you use to move the box? Answers will vary.

40

Procedure

1. Explain the concept of work. Tell students that we sometimes need help to do work. A machine is something that helps us do work. Ask students if they can think of any machines that are used in the classroom. Discuss their answers.

2. Have students put a red circle around all the objects on the worksheet that will help pull a box, and a blue circle around all the objects that will help push a box. If an object can do both, put both circles around the object. When students have circled all the objects, ask them to answer the questions at the bottom of the page.

Discovery Questions

- How can machines make work easier?
- What are some machines that help us in the house?
- What are some machines that help us outside?

Machine Mobile

Purpose

To identify the six main forms of simple machines.

Processes

Observing, comparing, grouping, and recording.

Materials

For each student:

- Activity worksheets, pages 41 and 42
- Crayons
- Scissors
- Six pieces of string of varying lengths
- Wire coat hanger

For the class:

- Glue
- Tape

Procedure

1. Explain that machines help us do work. Ask students if they can find any machines in the classroom. Then tell students that we call machines with no moving parts or one moving part simple machines. For instance, many tools that we use are simple machines. Point out various things in the classroom, such as a pencil, pencil sharpener, scissors, record player, or radio, and ask students to tell you if they have more than one moving part. Ask them which of the objects are simple machines.

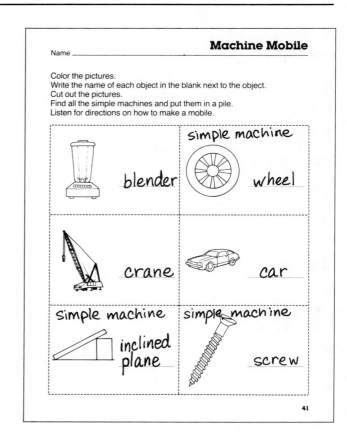

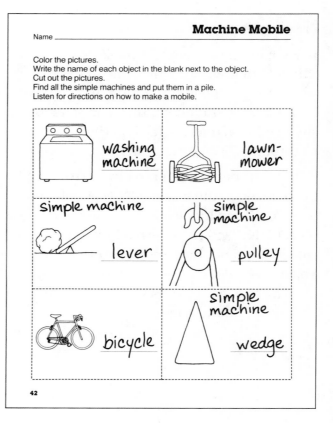

2. Duplicate worksheets on heavy paper. Have students write the name of each object in the blank next to the object. Then have them color and cut out the cards. Ask students to find all the cards that are simple machines and put them in one pile. Have them fold the simple-machine cards in half so the picture and the name are on the outside, and paste the two sides together with a piece of string between them. (See Figure A.) Then have them tape each piece of string onto the coat hanger to make a mobile. (See Figure B.)

Discovery Questions

- What are some simple machines in your house that are levers?
- What are some simple machines in your house that are screws?
- What are the simple machines that make up a wheelbarrow?

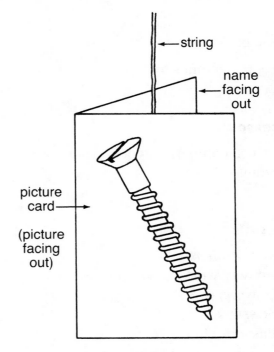

Figure A

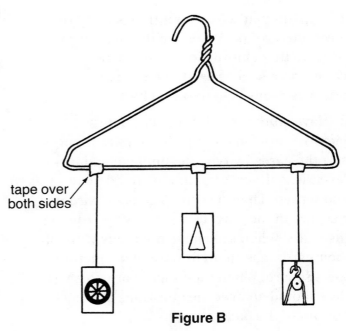

Figure B

Chart-a-Machine

Purpose

To group machines by types.

Processes

Observing, comparing types, grouping, and recording.

Materials

For each student:
- Activity worksheets, pages 43 and 44
- Crayons
- Scissors
- Paste or glue

Procedure

1. Explain that we can put things that are alike into groups. When we do this, we can observe them more closely and make comparisons more easily. One way to organize items is to make a chart.

2. Have students color and cut out the picture cards on page 43. Then have them sort the cards by type of simple machine—lever, wheel, screw, pulley, inclined plane, and wedge. They should place each card on a square in the correct machine-type row on the chart. When they have done this with all their cards, ask them to paste each picture to its square. When their charts are finished they should answer the questions at the bottom of the page.

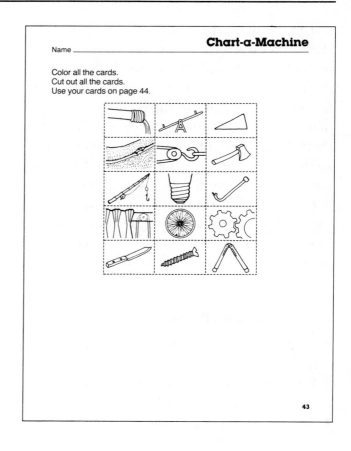

Name _____

Chart-a-Machine

Color all the cards.
Cut out all the cards.
Use your cards on page 44.

43

Discovery Questions

- How are screws and inclined planes alike?
- How are wheels and pulleys alike?
- How are wedges and inclined planes alike?

ACTIVITY WORKSHEETS

Name _____

Use one of the words to tell what each thing is.
Write the word below the picture.

solid   liquid   gas

milk 	book 	water 	ice 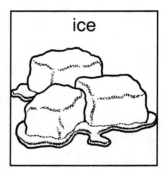

_____   _____   _____   _____

air 	rock 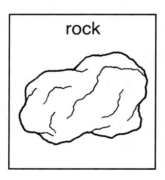	honey 	bubbles in  soda

_____   _____   _____   _____

Which thing on this page do you think is the heaviest? _____

Which thing on this page do you think is the lightest? _____

Explorations in Physical Science, © 1987 David S. Lake Publishers

Touch and Tell

Paste each item next to a letter.
Write its name.

A.   B.   C.   D.

_____   _____   _____   _____

Look at your texture cards.
Pick four cards that best describe how each item feels.
Paste the cards in the boxes below.

Item A	Item B	Item C	Item D

Name _____

Cut out the texture cards on this page.
Use your cards on page 23.

soft	soft	soft	soft
hard	hard	hard	hard
bumpy	bumpy	bumpy	bumpy
smooth	smooth	smooth	smooth
coarse	coarse	coarse	coarse
silky	silky	silky	silky
sticky	sticky	sticky	sticky
slick	slick	slick	slick

Name _____

Cut out the pictures.
Put the pictures in order.
Staple the pictures together on the line.
Flip the pages with your thumb and watch ice turn into steam!

Name _____

Color all the pictures.
Cut out the pictures.
Use your picture cards on page 27.

Explorations in Physical Science, © 1987 David S. Lake Publishers

Name _____

Put the objects that a magnet attracts in this box.	Put the objects that a magnet does not attract in this box.

How many objects are attracted by magnets? _____

How many objects are not attracted by magnets? _____

Graph-a-Magnet

Color all the magnets like this:

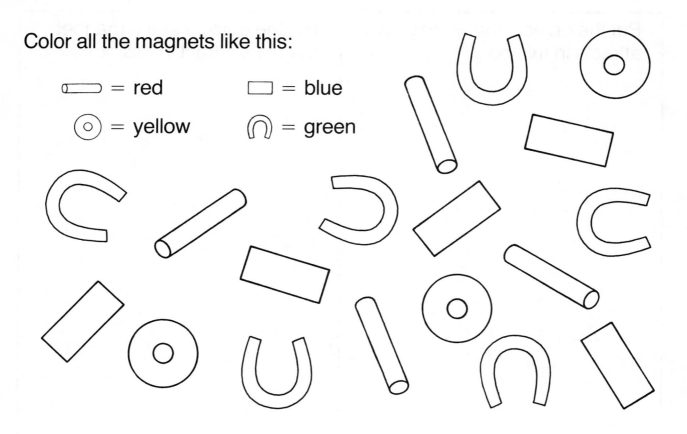

= red   = blue

= yellow   = green

Count all the magnets that are the same color.
Make a graph. For each magnet shape, color the number of boxes that
tells how many.

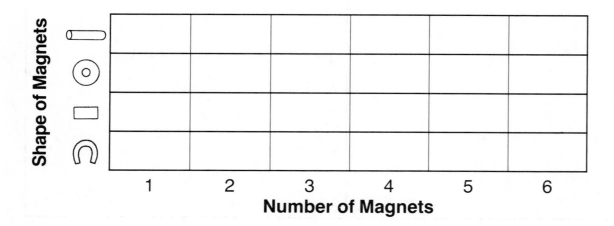

Shape of Magnets

Number of Magnets

Circle the shape that has the greatest number: ☐ ∩

Circle the shape that has the greatest number: ☐ ⊙

Explorations in Physical Science, © 1987 David S. Lake Publishers

Name _____

- Place two magnets on your desk.
  Put them together like this:

  | S   N | | N   S |

  Draw a picture in the box that shows what happens.

Did the magnets attract or repel each other? _____

- Put them together like this:

  | N   S | | S   N |

  Draw a picture in the box that shows what happens.

Did the magnets attract or repel each other? _____

- Put them together like this:

  | S   N | | S   N |

  Draw a picture in the box that shows what happens.

Did the magnets attract or repel each other? _____

Explorations in Physical Science, © 1987 David S. Lake Publishers

Name _____

Circle the picture that answers each question.

Test A: What happened when you put the two balloons together?

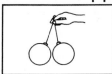 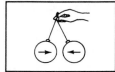 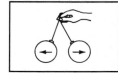

Test B: What happened when you put the rubbed balloons together?

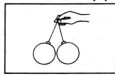 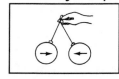 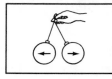

Test C: What happened when you put your hand between the balloons?

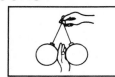 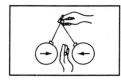 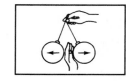

Test D: What happened when you held the two pieces of nylon together?

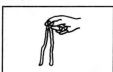  

Test E: What happened when you held the rubbed pieces of nylon together?

Test F: What happened when you put the rubbed piece of nylon next to the rubbed balloon?

 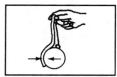 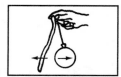

Explorations in Physical Science, © 1987 David S. Lake Publishers

Energy Circles

Name _____

Color the pictures.
Cut out the pictures.

Explorations in Physical Science, © 1987 David S. Lake Publishers

Energy Circles

Name _____

Color these cards yellow:

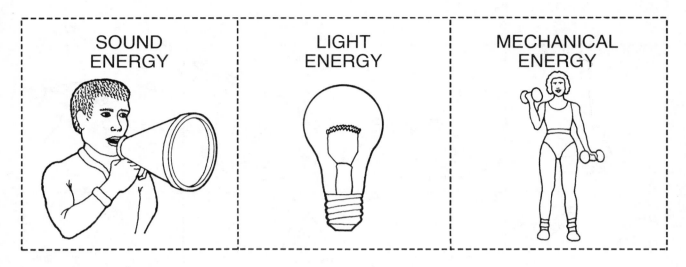

| SOUND ENERGY | LIGHT ENERGY | MECHANICAL ENERGY |

Color these cards red:

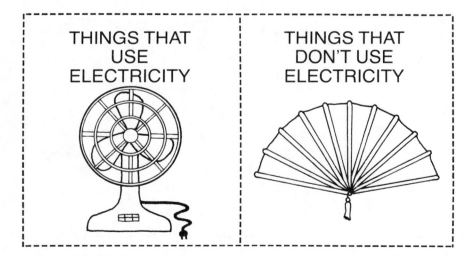

| THINGS THAT USE ELECTRICITY | THINGS THAT DON'T USE ELECTRICITY |

Cut out the cards.

Explorations in Physical Science, © 1987 David S. Lake Publishers

What Gives Us Light?

Look at each pair of pictures.
Read the sentence below the pair.
Circle the picture that the sentence describes.
Color the pictures.

This object gives us light during
   the day.

This object gives us light at night.

This object does not need
   electricity to give us light.

We see this light during a storm.

Explorations in Physical Science, © 1987 David S. Lake Publishers

Does Light Go Through?

Name _____

Think about each item on this page.

Do you think a flashlight can shine through it?

If you think a lot of light would shine through it, leave the first box blank like this: ☐

If you think a little light would shine through it, color the first box like this: ▨

If you think no light would shine through it, color the first box like this: ▧

When your teacher tests each item, mark what you see in the second box.

	Guess	Actual		Guess	Actual
Paper Towel	☐	☐	Plastic Wrap	☐	☐
Cardboard	☐	☐	Glass	☐	☐
Aluminum Foil	☐	☐	Wax Paper	☐	☐
Black Paper	☐	☐	Wood	☐	☐

Which things are opaque? _____

Which things are transparent? _____

Which things are translucent? _____

Explorations in Physical Science, © 1987 David S. Lake Publishers

Finding Shadow Lengths

Name _____

How are these shadows alike?
How are these shadows
    different?
Measure the length of each
    shadow in centimeters.
Record each length on the chart.

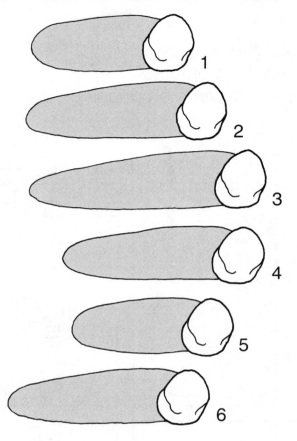

Shadow	Length (cm)
1	
2	
3	
4	
5	
6	

Color the boxes to show the number of shadows for each length.

Number of Shadows

	1	2	3	4	5
6					
5					
4					
3					
2					
1					

Length of Shadow (cm)

How many different lengths are there? _____

Which length has the most shadows? _____

Which shadow is unlike any other? _____

City Noises/Country Noises

Name _____

Color the objects.
Cut out the objects.
Use your cards on pages 37 and 38.

Explorations in Physical Science, © 1987 David S. Lake Publishers

Name _____

Put the objects that you would hear in the city in the picture below.
Paste the cards to make a scene.

Name _____

Put the objects that you would hear in the country in the picture below.
Paste the cards to make a scene.

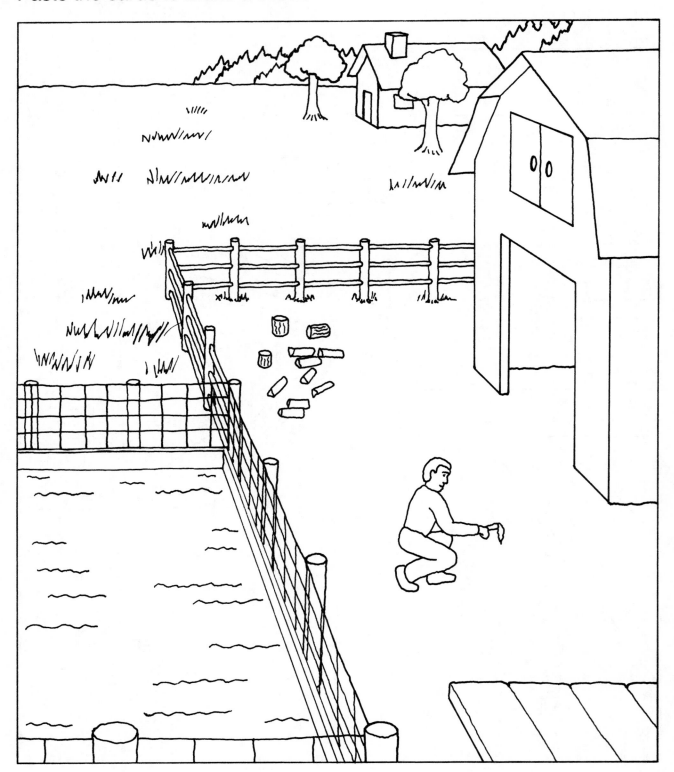

Explorations in Physical Science, © 1987 David S. Lake Publishers

Name _____

Color the pictures.
Put a green circle around all the things that make sounds we can hear.
Put a red circle around all the things that make sounds we cannot hear.
Put a blue circle around all the things that don't make sounds.

Moving Machines

Name _____

Sandy wants to move a box.
It is too heavy to lift.
Find all the objects in the pictures that could help Sandy move the box.
Put a red circle around the objects that would pull the box.
Put a blue circle around the objects that would push the box.

Are all the objects with circles around them machines?   yes   no

Look at the objects that are not circled. Which ones are machines?

_____

Which object would you use to move the box? _____

Explorations in Physical Science, © 1987 David S. Lake Publishers

Machine Mobile

Color the pictures.
Write the name of each object in the blank next to the object.
Cut out the pictures.
Find all the simple machines and put them in a pile.
Listen for directions on how to make a mobile.

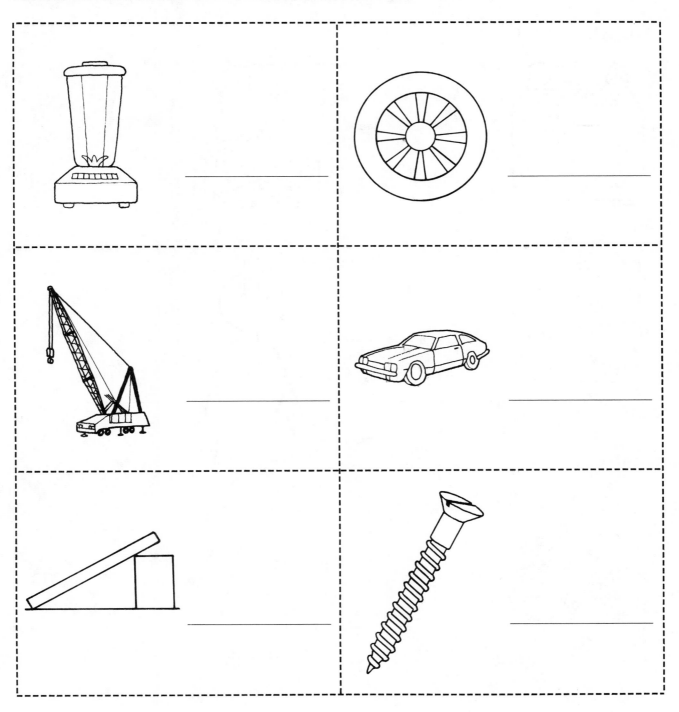

Explorations in Physical Science, © 1987 David S. Lake Publishers

Machine Mobile

Color the pictures.
Write the name of each object in the blank next to the object.
Cut out the pictures.
Find all the simple machines and put them in a pile.
Listen for directions on how to make a mobile.

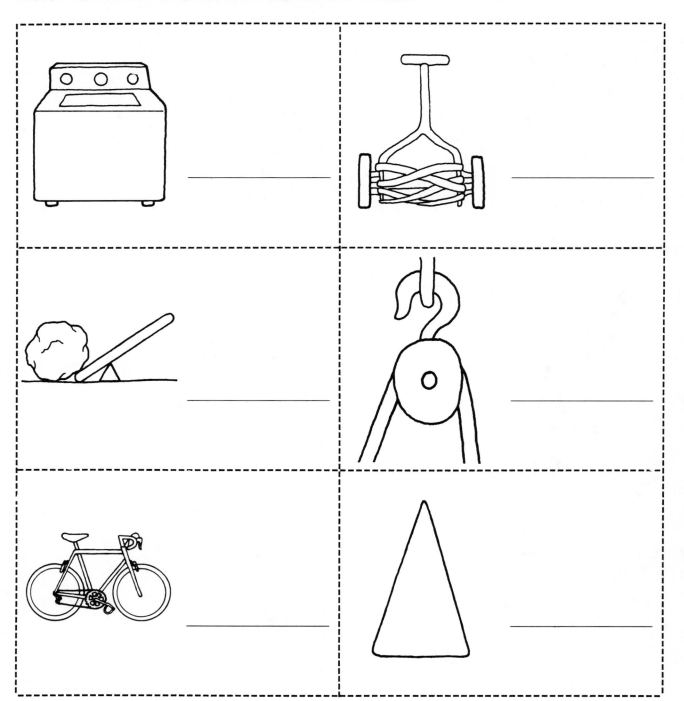

Explorations in Physical Science, © 1987 David S. Lake Publishers

Name _____

Color all the cards.
Cut out all the cards.
Use your cards on page 44.

Chart-a-Machine

Name _____

Look at all your cards.
Sort your cards into piles of the same machine type.
Put each card in a box that names its type.
Paste the cards down.

lever	lever	lever	lever	lever
pulley	pulley	pulley	pulley	pulley
screw	screw	screw	screw	screw
wheel	wheel	wheel	wheel	wheel
inclined plane	inclined plane	inclined plane	inclined plane	inclined plane
wedge	wedge	wedge	wedge	wedge

Which machine type has the most cards? _____

How many cards does it have? _____

Which machine type has the least cards? _____

How many cards does it have? _____

Doing Science

Explorations in Earth Science

Process-Oriented Activities for Grades 1–3

PART 3   EXPLORATIONS IN EARTH SCIENCE

CONTENTS

TEACHER'S GUIDE

Watching Weather

Purpose

To observe the weather daily for a week and to record the weather on a chart.

Processes

Observing, comparing, collecting data, recording, and reporting.

Materials

For each student:
- Activity worksheets, pages 22, 23, and 24
- Four envelopes
- Scissors
- Paste or glue
- Crayons

Watching Weather

Name _____

Write the starting date on the calendar.
Pick the cards that show what it is like outside.
Paste the cards in the boxes.

Month _____ Day _____ Year _____

	Monday	Tuesday	Wednesday	Thursday	Friday
Temperature					
Wind					
Clouds					
Precipitation					

24

Procedure

1. Briefly discuss temperature, wind, precipitation, and clouds. Ask students to look at pages 22 and 23. Explain that the pictures are symbols of different kinds of weather. Ask them to describe the type of weather each picture represents.

2. Have students write *temperature* on the first envelope, *wind* on the second, *precipitation* on the third, and *clouds* on the fourth. Then have students color and cut each group of cards on page 22 and 23. They should put the cards in the proper envelope. (If you want to give them grouping practice, don't ask them to cut out one group at a time. Instead, have them sort the pictures once they have finished coloring and cutting.)

3. Have students write the starting date on page 24. Have students observe the weather at the same time each day. After they observe each day, ask them to choose the symbols that best describe that day's weather. Have them paste the symbols in the appropriate boxes. When the week is over, ask them to share the information they have recorded.

Discovery Questions

- What causes the weather to change?
- Where is the sun on a cloudy or rainy day?
- Where do rain and snow come from?

Hot and Cold

Purpose

To practice recording temperatures on a thermometer.

Processes

Observing, interpreting, recording data, and reporting.

Materials

For each student:
- Activity worksheet, page 25
- Red crayon

For the class:
- Two basins of water, one hot and one cold
- Weather thermometer

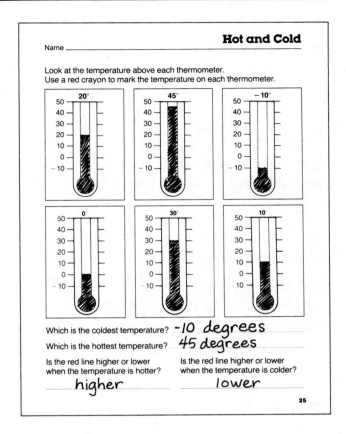

Procedure

1. Discuss thermometers and the way they work. Ask students the following kinds of questions:

What is temperature? (How hot or cold something is.)

What is inside a thermometer? (A liquid that is very sensitive to changes in temperature.)

How does a thermometer work? (The temperature makes the liquid inside of the tube go up or down.)

2. Put the thermometer in the basin with cold water. Show students how to read the result on the thermometer. Then place the thermometer in the basin with hot water.

Have children check the result again. Ask students if the liquid inside the thermometer goes up or down in the cold water. Then ask if it goes up or down in the hot water.

3. Have students use a red crayon to mark the temperature on the thermometers on the worksheet. They should also answer the questions at the bottom of the page.

Discovery Questions

- Are our bodies colder or warmer than the air around us?
- Why does a wet hand feel colder than a dry hand?

How Hot Is It?

Purpose

To measure and graph air temperatures.

Processes

Observing, comparing temperatures, measuring temperatures, graphing, and reporting.

Materials

For each student:
- Activity worksheet, page 26

For the class:
- Weather thermometer

Procedure

1. Attach a thermometer outside a classroom window. Make sure it is shielded from direct sunlight. Explain that we can find out what the temperature is outside by reading the thermometer.

2. Have students check the temperature once a day for a week. (They should check it at the same time each day.) Have them record their findings on the worksheet. At the end of a week, have them graph their results on the graph provided. This will show the general temperature change throughout the week. You may want to have students display their worksheets in the classroom.

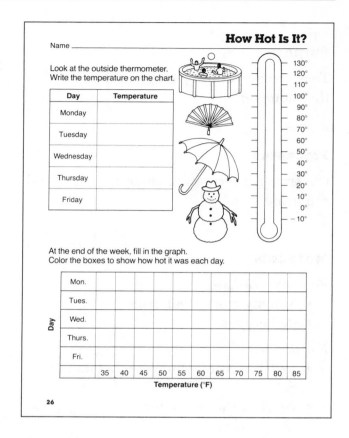

Discovery Questions

- What would happen if you put the thermometer in direct sunlight?
- Why would we want to measure the temperature at the same time each day?

Make a Balloon Rise!

Purpose

To show that hot air rises and can inflate a balloon.

Processes

Observing, comparing details, and sequencing.

Materials

For each student:
- Activity worksheet, page 27
- Scissors
- Stapler
- Crayons (optional)

For the class:
- Empty glass bottle with a long neck (soda bottles work well)
- Balloon
- Bucket of ice

Procedure

1. Pass the bottle around for students to feel. Then place it in the ice. Ask students how they think the bottle will feel when you take it out.

2. Stretch the neck of a deflated balloon around the neck of the cooled bottle. Pass the bottle around the class for the students to feel again. Ask them to tell you how the bottle feels. As the bottle is warmed by the children's hands, the balloon will start to inflate. (The air becomes warmer, and rises.)

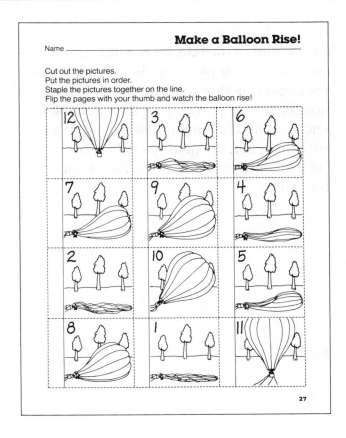

3. Place the bottle back into the ice. Have the students observe what happens. (The balloon will deflate as the air inside the bottle grows colder.) Have the students predict what would happen if you warmed the bottle again. Explain that as the air inside the bottle gets warm, it rises. When it rises, it fills up the balloon.

4. Duplicate the worksheet on heavy paper. Have students cut out the pictures on the worksheet. Then have students arrange the pictures to show the hot-air balloon inflating and rising. The picture of the deflated balloon should be on top of the pile, and the picture of the balloon in the air should be on

the bottom of the pile. Once students have sequenced their pictures, they should staple the pages together to form a booklet. By holding the stapled ends of the flip book in one hand and flipping the pages of the book with the other, the pictures will create a "movie." Students may color the pictures if they wish.

Discovery Questions

- How is the balloon on a bottle like a thermometer?
- Would a balloon rise if you filled it with cold air?
- What are some other ways to make a balloon rise?

Wind Wheels

Purpose

To introduce the concept of wind.

Processes

Observing, collecting data, comparing, drawing conclusions, and recording.

Materials

For each student:
- Activity worksheets, pages 28 and 29
- Scissors
- New pencil with eraser
- Tape
- Pushpin

Procedure

1. Duplicate page 28 on heavy paper. Have students cut out the pattern as indicated on the worksheet. Then have them tape the right corner of each triangle to the square as shown.

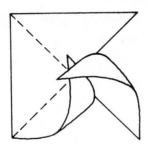

Help them insert a pin through the center of the paper to attach it to the eraser end of the pencil.

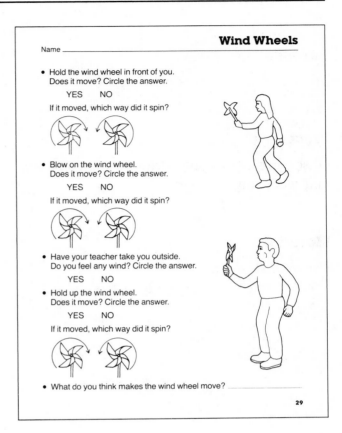

2. Have children follow directions on page 29. Make sure the wind wheels are held the same way throughout the experiment. When they are finished, explain that air is all around us. When we blow with our mouths or move our arms, the air moves. When the air moves it creates wind. This is what moves the wind wheel.

Discovery Questions

- What makes the wind wheel spin in only one direction?
- What happens to the wind wheel if there is a stronger wind?
- What happens to the wind wheel if there is no wind?

Is the Wind Blowing?

Purpose

To identify the effects of wind.

Processes

Observing, comparing, drawing conclusions, and recording.

Materials

For each student:

- Activity worksheet, page 30
- Crayons

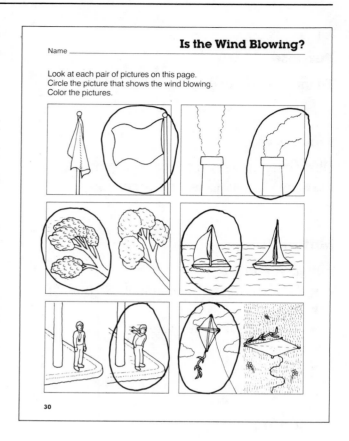

Procedure

1. Explain that wind is moving air. Ask students if they can see the wind. Discuss their answers. Then ask students to identify all the ways they can tell that the wind is blowing.

2. Tell students to look at the pairs of pictures on the worksheet and to circle the picture in each pair that shows the wind blowing. When they are finished, have them color the pictures.

Discovery Questions

- What could we use to tell what direction the wind is blowing?
- What things can only be done when there is a strong wind?
- What things cannot be done when there is a strong wind?

Cloudy Days

Purpose

To identify and classify different types of clouds.

Processes

Observing, comparing, classifying, and recording.

Materials

For each student:
- Activity worksheet, page 31
- Crayons (optional)

For the class:
- Pictures of stratus, cumulus, and cirrus clouds

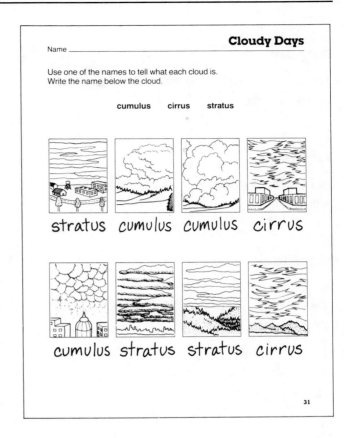

Name _____

Cloudy Days

Use one of the names to tell what each cloud is.
Write the name below the cloud.

cumulus   cirrus   stratus

stratus cumulus cumulus cirrus

cumulus stratus stratus cirrus

31

Procedure

1. Show students the pictures of the clouds. Ask them which clouds they have seen in the sky. Explain that there are three basic types of clouds—*stratus* clouds, which are flat and spread out across the sky like a blanket; *cumulus* clouds, which are usually rounded and puffy and look like cotton balls stuck together; and *cirrus* clouds, which look like feathery curls.

2. Have students write the general cloud type below each cloud shown on the worksheet. They may color the pictures if they wish.

Discovery Questions

- What types of clouds produce rain or snow?
- What types of clouds do you see today?

Weather Clothes

Purpose

To identify clothes that we wear in different types of weather.

Processes

Observing, comparing, classifying, and recording.

Materials

For each student:
- Activity worksheet, page 32
- Crayons

Procedure

1. Explain that we wear certain clothes in certain types of weather. Ask students to give you examples of clothes they would wear in hot weather, cold weather, dry weather, and wet weather.

2. Have the students color the pictures on the worksheet. Then have them put a green circle around all the clothes and items that are appropriate for rain, and put a blue circle around all the clothes and items that are appropriate for snow.

3. Answers on the student worksheets may vary depending on children's experiences with different climates.

Discovery Questions

- Why do you think we make many raincoats out of plastic?
- How does wearing a hat in the sun protect you?

Measuring Snowflakes

Purpose

To compare the widths of snowflakes.

Processes

Observing, comparing widths, collecting data, and graphing.

Materials

For each student:

- Activity worksheet, page 33
- Centimeter ruler
- Crayons

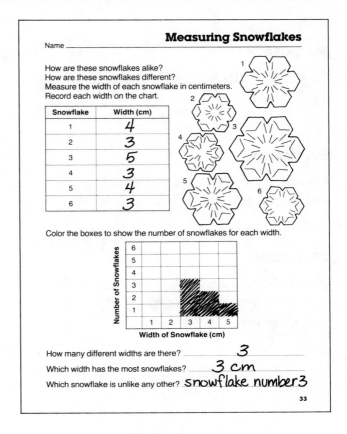

Measuring Snowflakes

Name _____

How are these snowflakes alike?
How are these snowflakes different?
Measure the width of each snowflake in centimeters.
Record each width on the chart.

Snowflake	Width (cm)
1	4
2	3
3	5
4	3
5	4
6	3

Color the boxes to show the number of snowflakes for each width.

How many different widths are there? _____ 3
Which width has the most snowflakes? _____ 3 cm
Which snowflake is unlike any other? snowflake number 3

33

Procedure

1. Explain that a group of objects that look alike may not all be exactly the same size. One way the size of such objects may differ is in width.

2. Have students measure the widths of the snowflakes on the worksheet. Then have them record the widths on the chart next to the snowflakes. After they have found the widths of all the snowflakes, they should complete the graph. When this is done they should answer the questions at the bottom of the page.

Discovery Questions

- What are some other ways we could find differences in size?
- What are some other ways that snowflakes differ from one another?
- What are snowflakes made of?

Graph-a-Rock

Purpose

To group rocks by shape, and to make and use a graph.

Processes

Observing, comparing shapes, classifying, recording, and reporting.

Materials

For each student:
- Activity worksheet, page 34
- Crayons

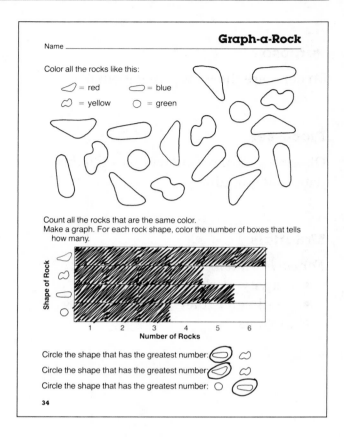

Procedure

1. Explain that objects have different shapes. Sometimes it is useful to group objects by their shapes. Ask students to describe different shapes that rocks have.

2. Have students color all the rocks on the worksheet with the suggested colors. Then have them complete the graph and answer the questions at the bottom of the page.

Discovery Questions

- Is there another way we could have grouped these rocks?
- How could we change a rock's shape?

Touch and Tell

Purpose

To describe rocks by their textures.

Processes

Observing, comparing textures, collecting data, recording, and reporting.

Materials

For each student:
- Activity worksheets, pages 35 and 36
- Three small rocks with different textures
  Examples: quartz
  granite
  lava (pumice)
  beach pebble
  crystal
  sandstone
- Scissors
- Paste or glue

Procedure

1. Explain that our fingers are very sensitive to touch. Our sense of touch helps us to gather information about objects. Tell students that we have a lot of different words to describe what we can feel. Ask students to name different textures, and discuss the textures listed on page 36.

2. Have students glue the three rocks next to the letters on page 35. Then have them cut out the description cards on page 36.

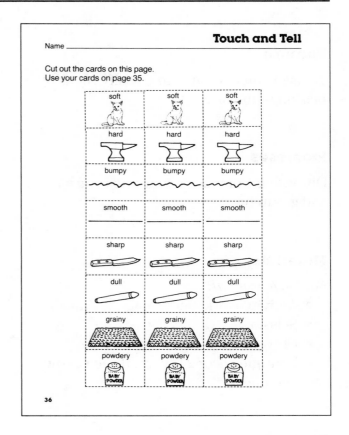

Tell them to close their eyes and feel the first rock. Ask them to choose the four description cards that best describe the texture of the first rock. They should then glue these cards in the boxes provided on page 35. Repeat the process for the remaining rocks.

Discovery Questions

- How does our sense of touch help us?
- What might different textures tell us about how the rock was formed?

Rock Circles

Purpose

To use Venn diagrams to classify rocks by markings and size.

Processes

Observing, comparing markings and size, and grouping.

Materials

For each student:
- Activity worksheets, pages 37 and 38
- Scissors
- Crayons
- Four pieces of 24″ yarn, three yellow and one red

Procedure

1. Duplicate the activity pages on heavy paper. Have students cut out the rock cards on page 37 and the label cards on page 38. Ask students to color the labels red or yellow as indicated on page 38. Next, have students tie the yarn into loops, so they each have three yellow loops and one red loop.

2. Ask students to put their red loops on their desks. Tell them to make the loop into the shape of a circle and put the red label LARGE ROCKS inside the circle. Then have them overlap the red circle with the three yellow circles so the circles look like Figure A.

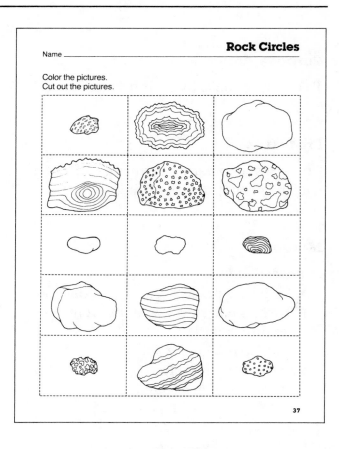

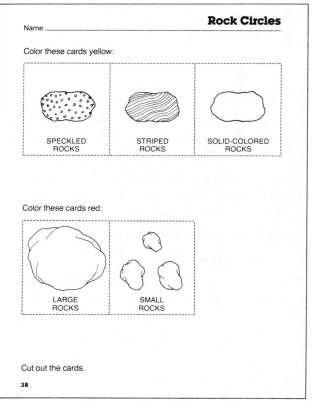

The labels SPECKLED ROCKS, STRIPED ROCKS, and SOLID-COLORED ROCKS should be placed in the yellow circles. Make sure the students put the yellow labels *outside* the areas of intersection between the yellow and red loops.

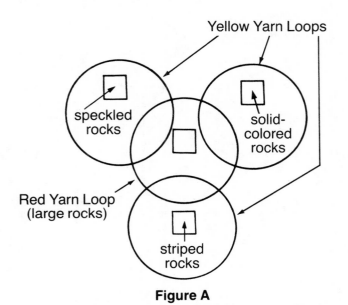

Figure A

3. Point out to students that the spaces where the red loop and the yellow loops overlap are called *intersections*. Tell them that these intersections are the places to put things that belong in both the red loop and one of the yellow loops. Have students group the rock cards by markings. Then have them put the cards in the appropriate yellow circles. Ask students to find the rocks in each yellow circle that are large. Tell them to move those cards into the intersection spaces. When they have finished the exercise, you might ask students to explain why we would want to organize the cards this way.

4. Repeat the exercise using the label SMALL ROCKS instead of the label LARGE ROCKS.

Discovery Questions

- What are some other ways to describe rocks?
- What is the difference between boulders and pebbles?
- What is sand made of?

Which Ones Are Rock?

Purpose

To identify things made out of rock.

Processes

Observing, comparing, grouping, recording, and reporting.

Materials

For each student:
- Activity worksheets, pages 39 and 40
- Scissors
- Paste or glue
- Crayons

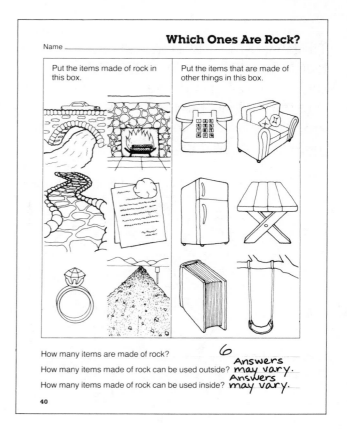

Which Ones Are Rock?

Name _____

Put the items made of rock in this box.

Put the items that are made of other things in this box.

How many items are made of rock? 6

How many items made of rock can be used outside? Answers may vary.

How many items made of rock can be used inside? Answers may vary.

40

Procedure

1. Explain that people can use rock to construct a variety of objects. Discuss some of the uses of rock. Ask students if they can name things made of rock in the classroom, outside, and at home.

2. Have students color and cut out the picture cards on page 39. Then, on page 40, have them sort the cards into two groups— items made of rock and items not made of rock. Once all the cards have been sorted, students should paste them on the page and answer the questions.

Discovery Questions

- Which would you use to build a chair— rock or wood?
- Which would you use to build a road— gravel or sticks?

Sorting Through Soil

Purpose

To identify objects that are part of soil.

Processes

Observing, comparing, inferring, recording, and reporting.

Materials

For each student:

- Activity worksheet, page 41
- Crayons
- Small cup of topsoil
- Hand lens

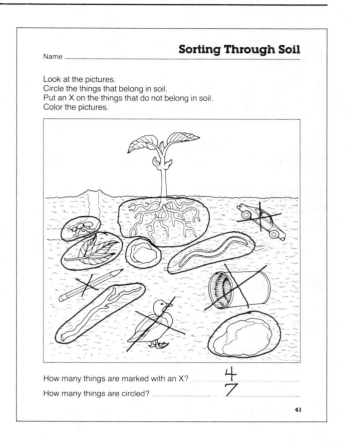

Name _____   **Sorting Through Soil**

Look at the pictures.
Circle the things that belong in soil.
Put an X on the things that do not belong in soil.
Color the pictures.

How many things are marked with an X? _____ 4
How many things are circled? _____ 7

41

Procedure

1. Give each student a small cup of topsoil and a hand lens. Ask them to look at the soil and name things that they see. Point out that there are living things in the soil such as leaves, bugs, and sticks, and that there are nonliving things in the soil such as rocks and sand. You might want to discuss pollution and its effects on the soil.

2. Have each student circle the things that belong in soil on the worksheet. They should mark the things that don't belong with an X. When they are finished they should answer the questions at the bottom of the page.

Discovery Questions

- How do earthworms help in soil?
- How do leaves help in soil?
- Why shouldn't we litter?

Soil Scientists

Purpose

To compare different soil types and how well suited they are for plant growth.

Processes

Observing, comparing, collecting data, recording, drawing conclusions, and reporting.

Materials

For each student:
- Activity worksheet, page 42
- Centimeter ruler
- Pencil

For each group of four students:
- One cup each of the following soil types:
  Sandy soil
  Potting soil
  Clay soil
- Three paper cups
- Three radish seeds
- Water
- Aluminum tray

Procedure

1. Divide the class into groups of four. Have each group poke a hole in the bottom of each cup, dampen the soil with water, and plant a seed in each cup. Have the students place the cups on the tray and put them in a place where they will get the same amount of light. Make sure students have labeled the cups.

2. Have the students observe the cups at the same time each day. Make sure they keep the soil damp but not wet. Have students measure the plant growth and record it on their worksheets. (Warn them not to press the ruler into the soil—this would give them inaccurate measurements.) At the end of ten days have students answer the questions at the bottom of the worksheet.

Discovery Questions

- How does soil help seeds grow?
- What would happen if you didn't water the seeds?
- What would happen if you didn't put the seeds in the sun?

Soil Scientists

Name _____

Follow the teacher's directions for planting your seeds.
Watch your plants for the next ten days.
Measure the plants each day.
Write down the height of the plant on the chart.

Day	Plant Height in Sandy Soil	Plant Height in Potting Soil	Plant Height in Clay Soil
1			
2			
3			
4			
5			
6			
7			
8			
9			
10			

After ten days, draw a picture on another piece of paper of how each plant looks.

Which soil grew the tallest plant? _____

Which soil grew the shortest plant? _____

Which soil seems to be the worst to grow plants in? _____

42

Soil Erosion Mobile

Purpose

To create a mobile that shows the sequence of soil erosion.

Processes

Observing, comparing, sequencing, and recording.

Materials

For each student:
- Activity worksheets, pages 43 and 44
- 20″ colored yarn or string
- Scissors
- Crayons
- Paste or glue

For the class:
- A pile of dry sand
- A basin
- A drinking straw
- Pictures showing wind erosion in the desert and on the plains

Procedure

1. Tell students you are going to blow on the sand with the drinking straw. Ask them to tell you what they think will happen. Blow through the straw and have the students observe the holes that the wind cuts into the sand.

2. Show students the pictures of the wind erosion. Discuss how the wind changed the land.

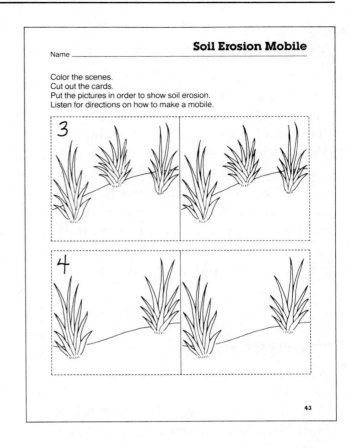

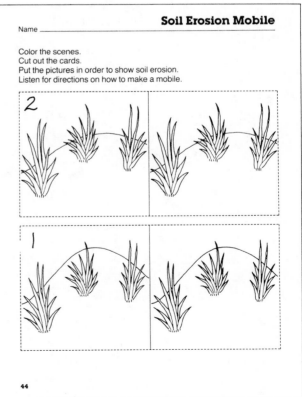

3. Duplicate the worksheets on heavy paper. Have students color and cut out the cards. They should arrange the cards on their desks with the dune at the top of the desk and the small bit of sand at the bottom of the desk. Have them fold the cards in half (with the pictures facing out) and glue the two sides together, making sure that the string is between them. (See Figure A.) They should put the picture of the dune at the top of the string and work their way down. They can then hang the mobile by its string.

Discovery Questions

- What are some other things that can erode the soil?
- Do you think it is easier for the wind to blow away loose sand or sand with plants on it?
- What are some ways to prevent soil erosion?

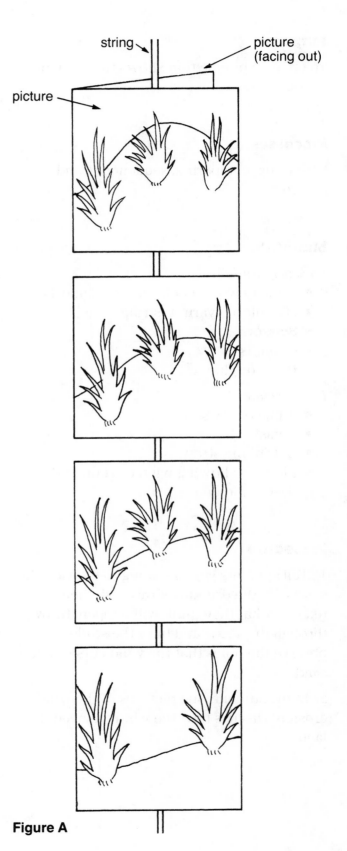

Figure A

ACTIVITY WORKSHEETS

Watching Weather

Cut out the cards.
Put them in the proper envelopes.
Use them on your weather chart.

Temperature

hot	hot	hot	hot	hot
cold	cold	cold	cold	cold
warm	warm	warm	warm	warm
cool	cool	cool	cool	cool

Clouds

cloudy	cloudy	cloudy	cloudy	cloudy
partly cloudy	partly cloudy	partly cloudy	partly cloudy	partly cloudy
foggy	foggy	foggy	foggy	foggy
sunny	sunny	sunny	sunny	sunny

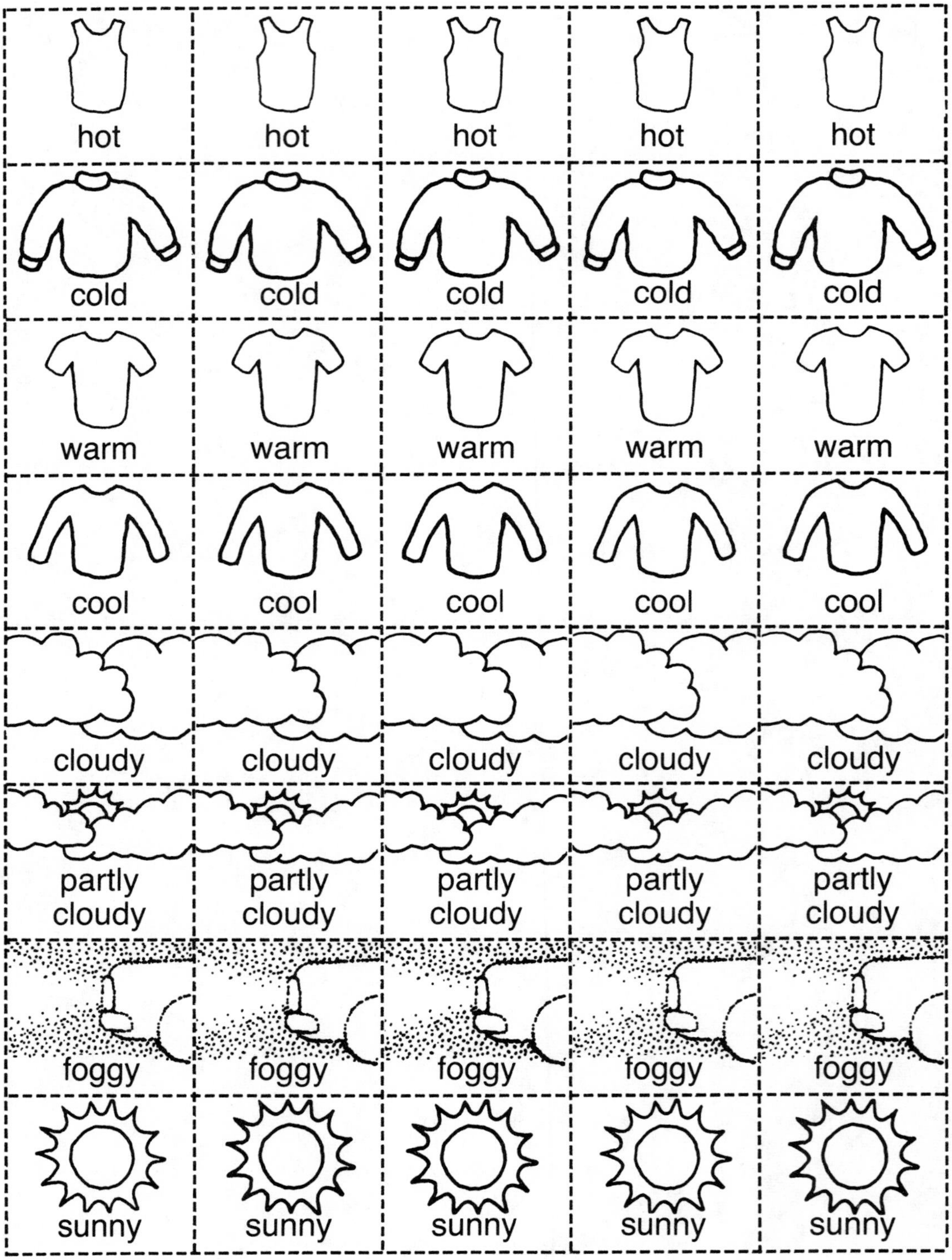

Explorations in Earth Science, © 1987 David S. Lake Publishers

Watching Weather

Name _____

Cut out the cards.
Put them in the proper envelopes.
Use them on your weather chart.

Precipitation

thunder-storm	thunder-storm	thunder-storm	thunder-storm	thunder-storm
rain	rain	rain	rain	rain
snow	snow	snow	snow	snow
hail	hail	hail	hail	hail

Wind

strong wind	strong wind	strong wind	strong wind	strong wind
medium wind	medium wind	medium wind	medium wind	medium wind
light breeze	light breeze	light breeze	light breeze	light breeze
no wind	no wind	no wind	no wind	no wind

Explorations in Earth Science, © 1987 David S. Lake Publishers

Name _____

Write the starting date on the calendar.
Pick the cards that show what it is like outside.
Paste the cards in the boxes.

Month _____ Day _____ Year _____					
	Monday	Tuesday	Wednesday	Thursday	Friday
Temperature					
Wind					
Clouds					
Precipitation					

Explorations in Earth Science, © 1987 David S. Lake Publishers

Name _____

Look at the temperature above each thermometer.
Use a red crayon to mark the temperature on each thermometer.

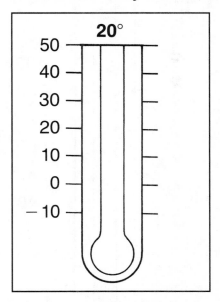

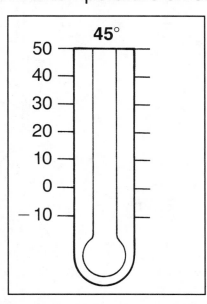

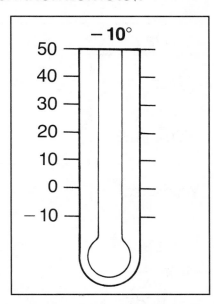

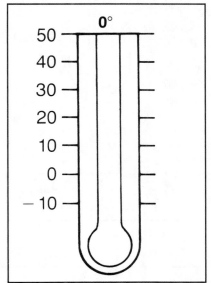

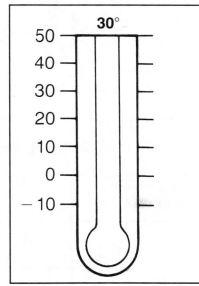

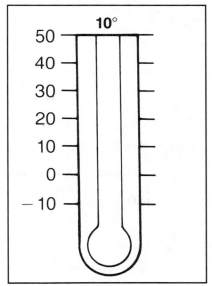

Which is the coldest temperature? _____

Which is the hottest temperature? _____

Is the red line higher or lower
when the temperature is hotter?

Is the red line higher or lower
when the temperature is colder?

_____

_____

How Hot Is It?

Name _____

Look at the outside thermometer.
Write the temperature on the chart.

Day	Temperature
Monday	
Tuesday	
Wednesday	
Thursday	
Friday	

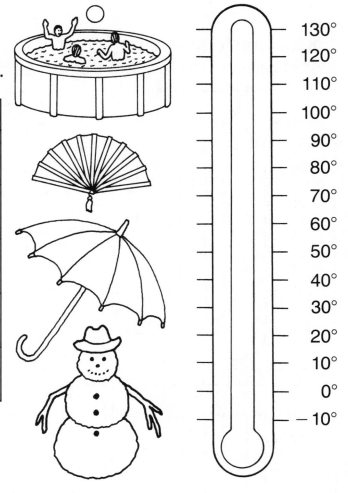

130°
120°
110°
100°
90°
80°
70°
60°
50°
40°
30°
20°
10°
0°
−10°

At the end of the week, fill in the graph.
Color the boxes to show how hot it was each day.

Day		35	40	45	50	55	60	65	70	75	80	85
	Mon.											
	Tues.											
	Wed.											
	Thurs.											
	Fri.											

Temperature (°F)

Explorations in Earth Science, © 1987 David S. Lake Publishers

Make a Balloon Rise!

Explorations in Earth Science, © 1987 David S. Lake Publishers

Name _____

Cut out the pictures.
Put the pictures in order.
Staple the pictures together on the line.
Flip the pages with your thumb and watch the balloon rise!

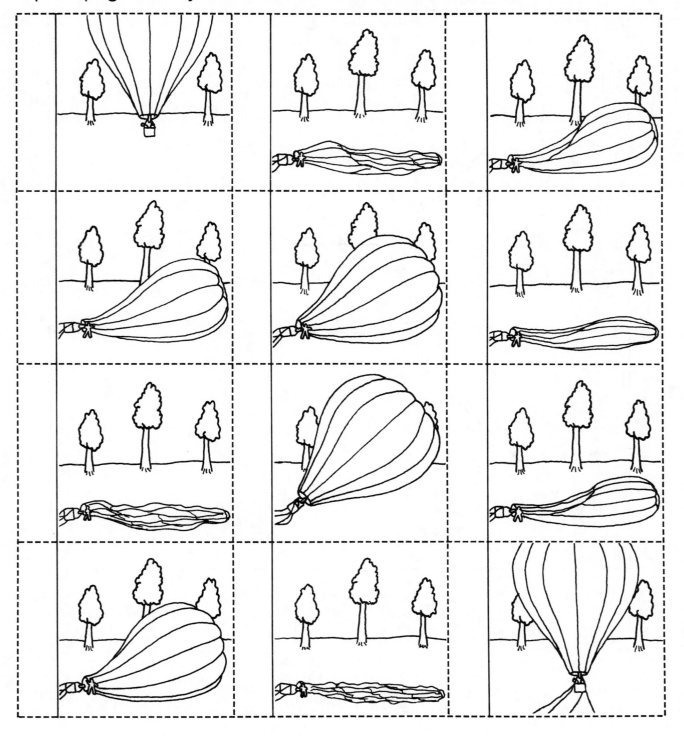

Name _____

Cut along the dotted lines.
Listen for directions on how to make a wind wheel.

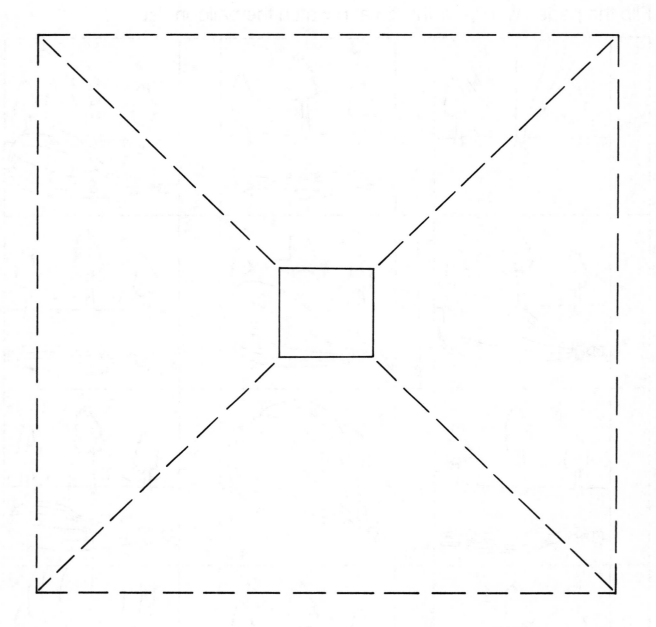

Wind Wheels

- Hold the wind wheel in front of you.
  Does it move? Circle the answer.

  YES   NO

  If it moved, which way did it spin?

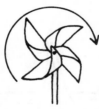 

- Blow on the wind wheel.
  Does it move? Circle the answer.

  YES   NO

  If it moved, which way did it spin?

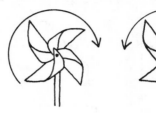

- Have your teacher take you outside.
  Do you feel any wind? Circle the answer.

  YES   NO

- Hold up the wind wheel.
  Does it move? Circle the answer.

  YES   NO

  If it moved, which way did it spin?

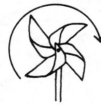 

- What do you think makes the wind wheel move? _____

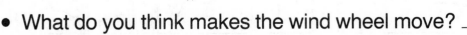

Explorations in Earth Science, © 1987 David S. Lake Publishers

Is the Wind Blowing?

Name _____

Look at each pair of pictures on this page.
Circle the picture that shows the wind blowing.
Color the pictures.

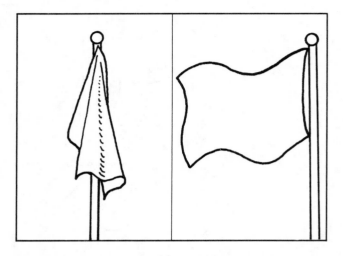

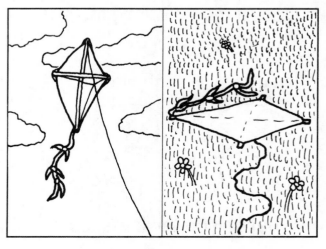

Explorations in Earth Science, © 1987 David S. Lake Publishers

Name _____

Use one of the names to tell what each cloud is.
Write the name below the cloud.

cumulus   cirrus   stratus

_____ _____ _____ _____

 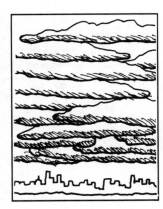 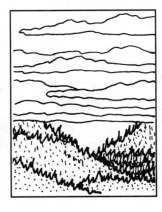 

_____ _____ _____ _____

Name _____

Color the pictures.
Put a green circle around all the items we would use in rainy weather.
Put a blue circle around all the items we would use in snowy weather.

Measuring Snowflakes

Name _____

How are these snowflakes alike?
How are these snowflakes different?
Measure the width of each snowflake in centimeters.
Record each width on the chart.

Snowflake	Width (cm)
1	
2	
3	
4	
5	
6	

Color the boxes to show the number of snowflakes for each width.

Number of Snowflakes	1	2	3	4	5
6					
5					
4					
3					
2					
1					

Width of Snowflake (cm)

How many different widths are there? _____

Which width has the most snowflakes? _____

Which snowflake is unlike any other? _____

Graph-a-Rock

Name _____

Color all the rocks like this:

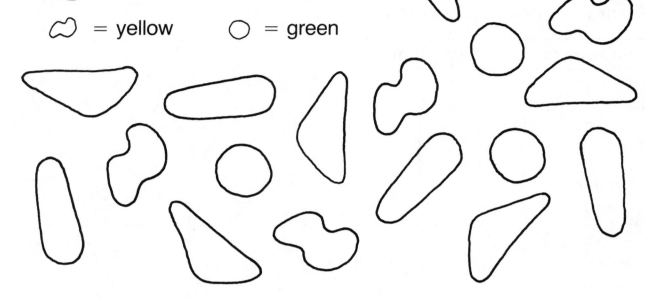

= red   = blue

= yellow   = green

Count all the rocks that are the same color.
Make a graph. For each rock shape, color the number of boxes that tells
    how many.

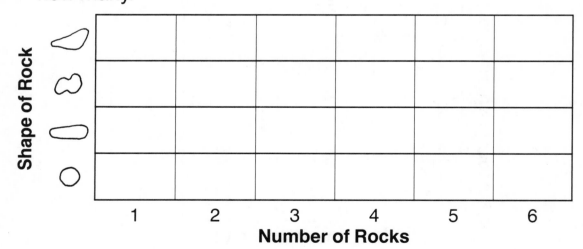

Shape of Rock

| | 1 | 2 | 3 | 4 | 5 | 6 |

Number of Rocks

Circle the shape that has the greatest number:

Circle the shape that has the greatest number:

Circle the shape that has the greatest number:

Explorations in Earth Science, © 1987 David S. Lake Publishers

Touch and Tell

Name ______________________________

Paste each item next to a letter.

A. ____________ B. ____________ C. ____________

Look at your texture cards.
Pick four cards that best describe how each item feels.
Paste the cards in the boxes below.

Item A	Item B	Item C

Name _____

Cut out the cards on this page.
Use your cards on page 35.

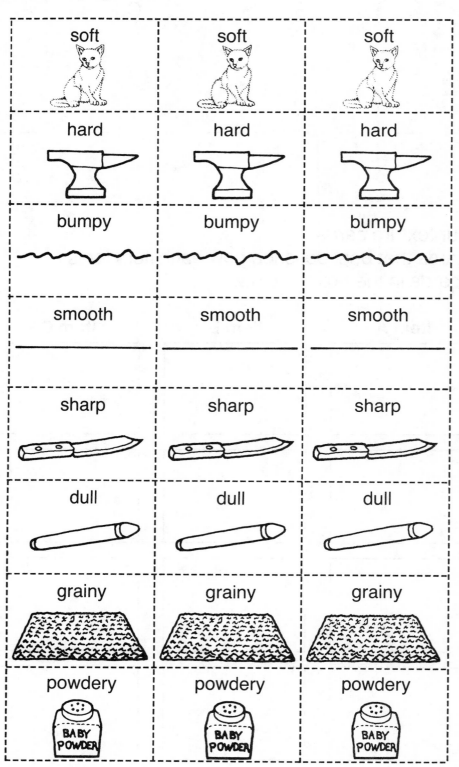

soft	soft	soft
hard	hard	hard
bumpy	bumpy	bumpy
smooth	smooth	smooth
sharp	sharp	sharp
dull	dull	dull
grainy	grainy	grainy
powdery	powdery	powdery

BABY POWDER

Explorations in Earth Science, © 1987 David S. Lake Publishers

Rock Circles

Color the pictures.
Cut out the pictures.

Name _____

Color these cards yellow:

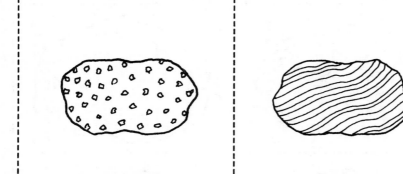

SPECKLED
ROCKS

STRIPED
ROCKS

SOLID-COLORED
ROCKS

Color these cards red:

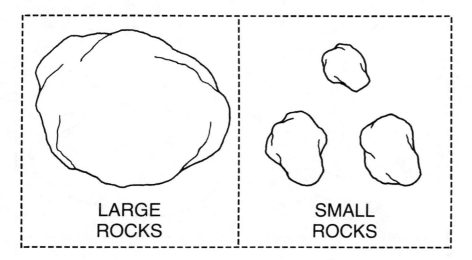

LARGE
ROCKS

SMALL
ROCKS

Cut out the cards.

Explorations in Earth Science, © 1987 David S. Lake Publishers

Which Ones Are Rock?

Name _____

Color all the pictures.
Cut out all the pictures.
Use your picture cards on page 40.

Name _____

Put the items made of rock in this box.	Put the items that are made of other things in this box.

How many items are made of rock? _____

How many items made of rock can be used outside? _____

How many items made of rock can be used inside? _____

Name _____

Look at the pictures.
Circle the things that belong in soil.
Put an X on the things that do not belong in soil.
Color the pictures.

How many things are marked with an X? _____

How many things are circled? _____

Soil Scientists

Name _____

Follow the teacher's directions for planting your seeds.
Watch your plants for the next ten days.
Measure the plants each day.
Write down the height of the plant on the chart.

Day	Plant Height in Sandy Soil	Plant Height in Potting Soil	Plant Height in Clay Soil
1			
2			
3			
4			
5			
6			
7			
8			
9			
10			

After ten days, draw a picture on another piece of paper of how each
plant looks.

Which soil grew the tallest plant? _____

Which soil grew the shortest plant? _____

Which soil seems to be the worst to grow plants in? _____

Explorations in Earth Science, © 1987 David S. Lake Publishers

Name _____

Color the scenes.
Cut out the cards.
Put the pictures in order to show soil erosion.
Listen for directions on how to make a mobile.

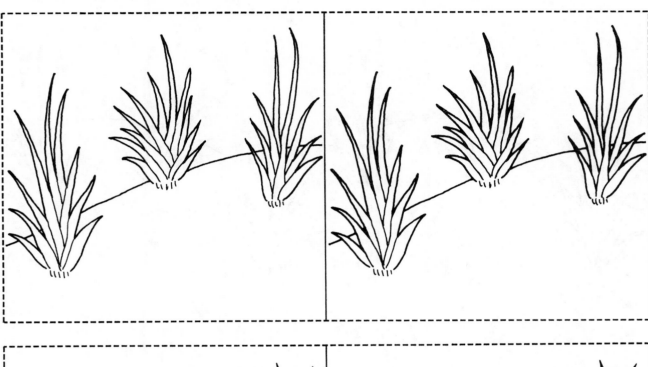

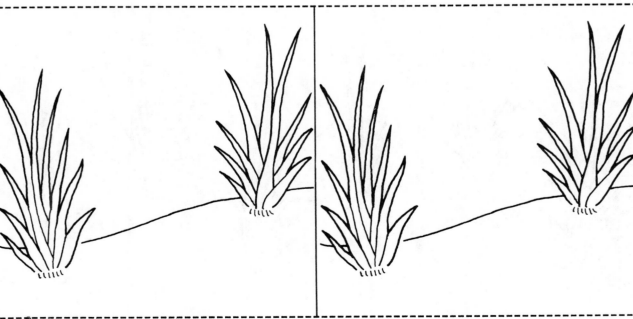

Name _____

Color the scenes.
Cut out the cards.
Put the pictures in order to show soil erosion.
Listen for directions on how to make a mobile.

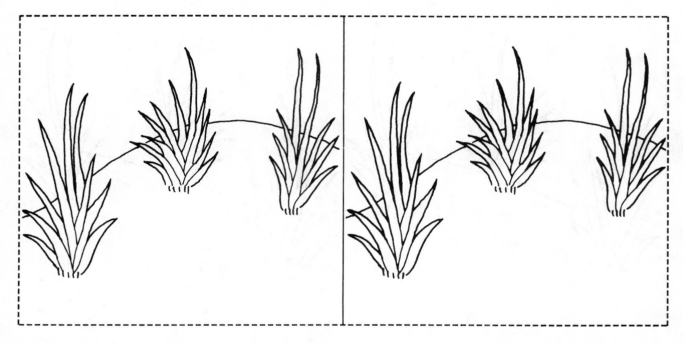

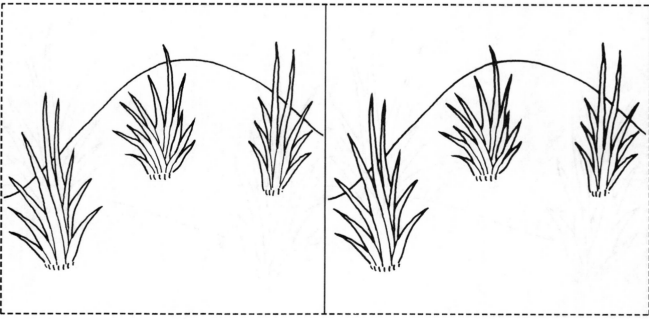

Explorations in Earth Science, © 1987 David S. Lake Publishers

Doing Science

Adventures in
Life Science

Process-Oriented Activities for Grades 4–6

PART 4   ADVENTURES IN LIFE SCIENCE

CONTENTS

TEACHER'S GUIDE

UFO (Unidentified Flowering Object)

Concept

Flowering plants can be classified as monocots or dicots.

Process Emphasis

Classifying

Materials

For each student:
- Activity worksheet, page 24
- Pen or pencil

For the class:
- Soaked corn kernels and lima beans

UFO (Unidentified Flowering Object)

Name _____

Identify the flowering plants below. Examine the pictures and decide whether each plant is a monocot or a dicot. Write *monocot* or *dicot* on the line under each plant. (Hint: Count the number of petals and look at the vein patterns in the leaves.)

| lily of the valley | petunia | round-leafed violet |
| monocot | dicot | dicot |

| daisy | daffodil | California poppy |
| monocot | monocot | dicot |

| orchid | geranium |
| monocot | dicot |

24

Procedure

1. Have students split open the corn kernels and the lima beans. Have them observe how different the two kinds of seeds look from each other. (The lima beans have two parts and open easily. The corn kernels have one part and do not open easily.) Explain that a lima bean is an example of a *dicot*. Dicots have two seed leaves, petals in multiples of four or five, and net-veined leaves. The corn kernel is an example of a *monocot*. Monocots have one seed leaf, petals in multiples of three, and veins in lines.

2. Hand out the worksheet. Have students classify the monocots and the dicots on the page.

Discovery Questions

- Why are many flowering plants important to people?
- Grasses are classified as flowering plants. Do you think they are monocots or dicots?

Dissect a Flower!

Concept

Flowers have different parts.

Process Emphasis

Observing and collecting data

Materials

For each student:
- Activity worksheet, page 25
- Pencil or crayons
- Sheet of newspaper
- Large simple flower, such as a lily or a tulip
- Hand lens

For the class:
- Pictures of different flowers

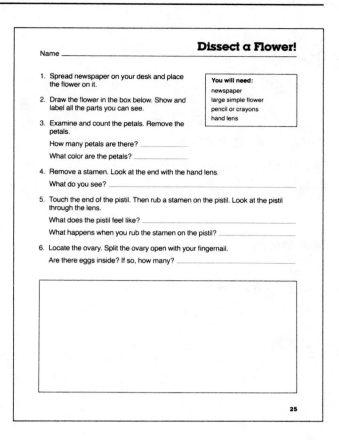

Name _____

Dissect a Flower!

1. Spread newspaper on your desk and place the flower on it.

2. Draw the flower in the box below. Show and label all the parts you can see.

3. Examine and count the petals. Remove the petals.

   How many petals are there? _____

   What color are the petals? _____

4. Remove a stamen. Look at the end with the hand lens.

   What do you see? _____

5. Touch the end of the pistil. Then rub a stamen on the pistil. Look at the pistil through the lens.

   What does the pistil feel like? _____

   What happens when you rub the stamen on the pistil? _____

6. Locate the ovary. Split the ovary open with your fingernail.

   Are there eggs inside? If so, how many? _____

You will need:
newspaper
large simple flower
pencil or crayons
hand lens

25

Procedure

1. Draw a diagram of the flower parts on the board (see Figure A). Discuss the structure of a flower with students. (You might also want to discuss the functions of the flower parts.) Show the pictures and ask students to find the flower parts in each picture. Point out that not all flowers have all the parts.

2. Hand out the worksheet and materials. Guide students through the directions on the worksheet.

Discovery Questions

- Are the flower parts located in the same places on each flower?
- Which parts of the flower are most important for producing seeds?

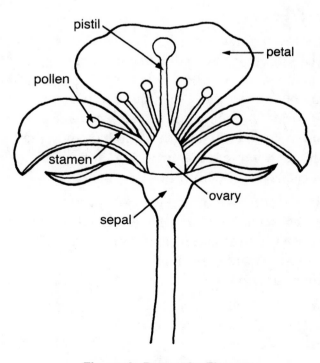

Figure A: Parts of a Flower

A Nutty Graph

Concept

Variations can be observed and measured.

Process Emphasis

Measuring, collecting data, and organizing data

Materials

For each student:

- Activity worksheet, page 26
- Ten peanuts in the shell
- Centimeter ruler
- Pencil

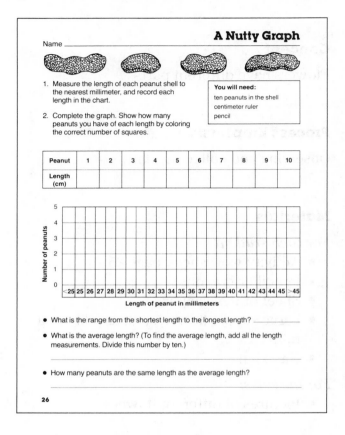

Procedure

1. Have students measure each of their peanuts (make sure they measure the peanut shell, not the seeds inside). You might need to show them how to measure accurately. Once students have measured and recorded the length of each peanut, they should complete the graph and answer the questions at the bottom of the page.

2. Ask students if they were surprised at the differences in length. Discuss variations and how variations can provide organisms with certain advantages in different environments.

Discovery Questions

- What would be the advantage of growing long peanuts?
- What would be the advantage of growing short peanuts?

Hitchhikers, Floaters, and Flyers

Concept

Seeds can be dispersed in several ways.

Process Emphasis

Collecting data and organizing data

Materials

For each student:
- Activity worksheet, page 27

For each group of four students:
- An assortment of seeds
  Examples:
    Hitchhikers—burrs
    Floaters—water-lily seeds
    Flyers—dandelion seeds, maple
        seeds
- Pint-size container filled with water
- Square of soft, fuzzy cloth
- Paste or glue

Procedure

1. Show students the different seeds and let them observe the seeds' sizes, shapes, and textures. Ask students to tell you what would happen if the seeds from a dandelion fell to the ground right next to the stalk rather than drifting away from the plant.

2. Divide the class into groups of four. Give each group an assortment of seeds. Have

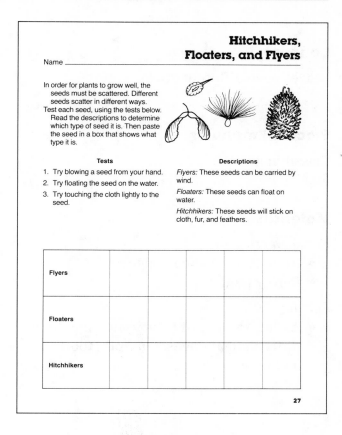

students test the seeds to determine the seeds' methods of dispersal. After the students have tested each type of seed, they should paste the seed in the appropriate square on the worksheet.

Discovery Questions

- Why is seed dispersal important to plants?
- How are coconut seeds dispersed?
- How are strawberry seeds dispersed?

At the Edge

Concept

Leaves have different edges.

Process Emphasis

Classifying

Materials

For each student:
- Activity worksheet, page 28
- Pen or pencil

For the class:
- An assortment of leaves showing three different leaf edges: (smooth, toothed, and lobed)

Name _____

At the Edge

If you look at a lot of different leaves, you will notice the leaves have different types of edges. Use the samples below to name the edge pattern for each leaf. Write *smooth, toothed,* or *lobed* on the blank under each leaf.

smooth   toothed   lobed

sassafras   chestnut   alder
lobed   toothed   smooth

live oak   California oak   willow
smooth   lobed   toothed

28

Procedure

1. Show students the leaves. Call attention to the different leaf edges. Explain that there are many different leaf edges. Discuss the edges of the leaves you are showing.

2. Hand out the worksheet. Have students identify the type of edge on each leaf. They should write the type of edge on the line provided.

Discovery Questions

- What are some other ways to classify leaves?
- How many different vein patterns can you see in leaves?
- What are some of the different shapes you can see in leaves?

The Edible Parts

Concept

We eat a variety of plant parts.

Process Emphasis

Grouping

Materials

For each student:
- Activity worksheet, page 29
- Pen or pencil

For the class:
- Variety of fruits, vegetables, herbs, and spices

Procedure

1. Show students the different foods. Ask them what all the items have in common. (They are things we eat. They are plants or plant parts.) Discuss the different plant parts, and ask students to identify which plant part each item is.

2. Hand out the worksheet. Ask students to list as many items as they can for each category on the page.

Discovery Questions

- Why don't we eat all plants?
- What are some plants that have parts we eat that also have poisonous parts that we don't eat?

Do Plants Breathe?

Concept

Energy is released in respiration.

Process Emphasis

Measuring, collecting data, and organizing data

Materials

For each student:
- Activity worksheet, page 30
- Pen or pencil

For each group of five students:
- Two thick glass jars
- Two thermometers
- Two rubber bands
- Two sheets of paper
- Cotton balls
- Water
- Bean sprout seeds (mung beans)
- Boiled bean sprout seeds

Procedure

1. Explain that food alone cannot provide all the energy that living organisms need. Ask students if they know how organisms get the extra energy. Discuss their answers and explain the process of respiration. Point out that some of the energy is released as heat.

2. Divide the class into groups of five. Hand out the materials to each group. Guide the

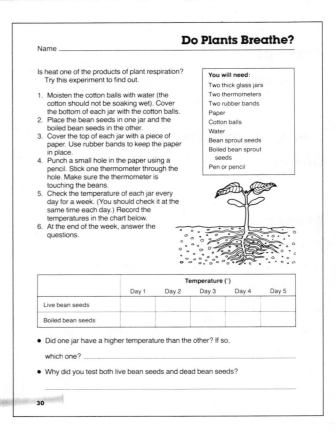

students through the directions on the worksheet. Have students check the temperatures of the jars at the same time each day for a week. When the week is over they should answer the questions at the bottom of the page.

Discovery Questions

- How is respiration related to photosynthesis?
- What are some other products of respiration?

Populations by a Pond

Concept

A population is a group of organisms of the same kind that live in a place at the same time.

Process Emphasis

Organizing data and drawing conclusions

Materials

For each student:
- Activity worksheet, page 31
- Colored pencils or crayons

Procedure

1. Ask students to tell you what the word *population* means to them. Discuss their answers and explain the definition of *population*. Have students list as many animal and plant populations as they can. You might also discuss the factors that affect the size of a population (food, predators, and weather).

2. Hand out the worksheet. Have students make bar graphs using the information provided. Ask them to use a different color for each population. They should also answer the questions at the bottom of the page.

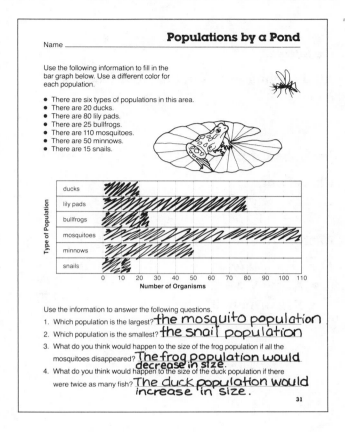

Populations by a Pond

Name _____

Use the following information to fill in the bar graph below. Use a different color for each population.

- There are six types of populations in this area.
- There are 20 ducks.
- There are 80 lily pads.
- There are 25 bullfrogs.
- There are 110 mosquitoes.
- There are 50 minnows.
- There are 15 snails.

Use the information to answer the following questions.

1. Which population is the largest? *the mosquito population*
2. Which population is the smallest? *the snail population*
3. What do you think would happen to the size of the frog population if all the mosquitoes disappeared? *The frog population would decrease in size.*
4. What do you think would happen to the size of the duck population if there were twice as many fish? *The duck population would increase in size.*

31

Discovery Questions

- What might change the size of a population?
- Why does the size of a population normally remain about the same size?
- What are some of the populations in your area?

Living Spaces

Concept

All the living things in one area make up a community.

Process Emphasis

Classifying

Materials

For each student:
- Activity worksheet, page 32
- Pen or pencil

Procedure

1. Have students compare the living things in two different areas of your school (for example, a cut lawn, a field with tall grass, or a vacant lot). Discuss where there is a greater diversity of organisms. Explain the meaning of the term *community*. Ask students to name the organisms that make up a specific community, such as a seashore or a forest.

2. Hand out the worksheet. Have students write the community—forest or pond—to which each animal belongs.

Discovery Questions

- What might happen to a pond community if the pond started to dry up?
- What might happen to a forest community if all the predators disappeared?

Food Chains

Concept

There is a feeding order among organisms in every community. This order is represented by a food chain.

Process Emphasis

Sequencing

Materials

For each student:
- Activity worksheet, page 33
- Pen or pencil

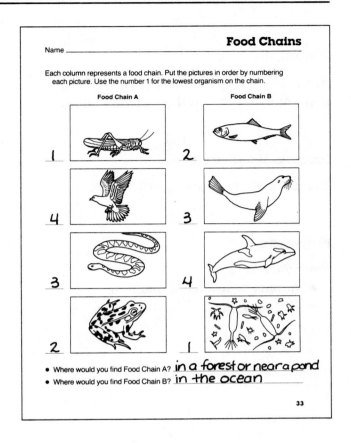

Procedure

1. Explain that a food chain illustrates the feeding order among organisms—it can be described as a pattern of who eats whom. Discuss the sequence of food chains—they begin with plants (producers), and then move on to plant eaters (herbivores), and finally end with either meat eaters (carnivores) or meat and plant eaters (omnivores). You might use the example of a ranch community. The chain begins with clover, moves on to cattle, and ends with people.

2. Hand out the worksheet. Ask students to show the order of a food chain by numbering the pictures correctly.

Discovery Questions

- What would happen if one of the elements of a food chain disappeared?
- Why are plants at the bottom of a food chain?

Survival Specialists

Concept

Animals have specialized body parts that help them survive in their environment.

Process Emphasis

Comparing and drawing conclusions

Materials

For each student:
- Activity worksheet, page 34
- Pen or pencil

Survival Specialists

Name _____

Many animals have special body parts that help them survive in their environments. Read the descriptions of the animals. Next to each picture, write the letter of the correct description of the animal.

A. This animal uses its handlike paws to catch fish and frogs.

B. The pointed beak on this animal allows it to dig under tree bark for insects.

C. This animal uses echos to find and eat insects in the air.

D. The long, curved claws of this animal allow it to dig tunnels to look for rodents.

E. This animal uses its sharp teeth to crack nuts.

1. E

2. D

3. C

4. B

5. A

34

Procedure

1. Discuss how the characteristics of some animals help them compete for scarce resources such as food, water, and space. Ask students if they can identify how certain body parts might help animals get the resources they need. Discuss their answers.

2. Hand out the worksheet. Have students read the descriptions of the body parts and how they help the animal. Have students match each description to the animal it describes.

Discovery Questions

- Why are some animals more successful than others in competing for resources?
- Do we have any specialized body parts that help us in our environment? If so, what are they?

Camouflage It!

Concept

Camouflage can help organisms survive in certain environments.

Process Emphasis

Comparing and drawing conclusions

Materials

For each student:
- Activity worksheet, page 35
- Pen or pencil

For the class:
- Scraps of different colored paper

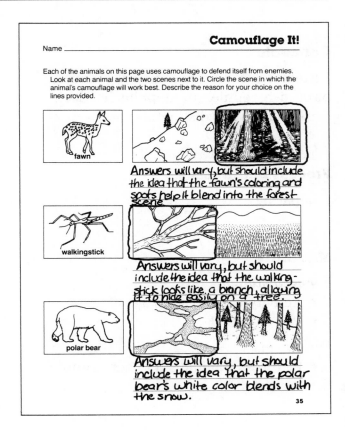

Procedure

1. Explain that many animals have particular colors, patterns, or shapes that protect them from enemies. Have students take different colored scraps of paper outside and scatter them in a defined area. Ask the students to find the scraps. Then have them tell you which colors were the easiest to locate and which colors were the hardest to locate. Point out that the colors of paper are like certain adaptations in animals.

2. Hand out the worksheet. Ask students to circle the environment in which each animal's camouflage will work best. Have students describe the reasons for their choices.

Discovery Questions

- What are some other ways in which animals protect themselves?
- How are the defenses of animals that live in groups different from those of animals that do not?

What's the Difference?

What's the Difference?

Name _____

All of the animals on this page are vertebrates (animals with backbones). In each row, circle the animal that does not belong with the rest. Then explain the reason for your choice on the line.

Answers will vary. (Ostrich is not a mammal.)

Answers will vary. (Cow is not a reptile.)

Answers will vary. (Dolphin is not a fish.)

Answers will vary. (Frog is not a reptile.)

36

Concepts

Vertebrates can be classified as mammals, birds, fish, reptiles, or amphibians. Each classification has distinctive traits.

Process Emphasis

Comparing

Materials

For each student:
- Activity worksheet, page 36
- Pen or pencil

For the class:
- Pictures of animals for each group of vertebrates

Procedure

1. Show students the pictures. Ask them if they know how scientists would group these animals. Discuss their answers. Then explain the characteristics of each vertebrate group. You might discuss why various animals are classified as they are. For instance, dolphins have hair, lungs, and give milk like other mammals. Also point out the differences between cold-blooded and warm-blooded animals.

2. Hand out the worksheet. Ask students to choose the animal in each row that does not belong with the rest. Make sure they explain the difference on the lines provided.

Discovery Questions

- Why would reptiles be more abundant in warm climates than in cold climates?
- What do reptiles and amphibians have in common?

Classification Circles

Concept

Animals can be classified in many ways.

Process Emphasis

Grouping

Materials

For each student:

- Activity worksheets, pages 37 and 38
- Scissors
- Four pieces 24″ yarn; three yellow and one red

Procedure

1. Duplicate the worksheets on heavy paper and hand out. Have students color the labels on page 37 according to the directions. They should cut out the cards and labels on both pages.

2. Ask students to tie each piece of yarn into a loop. They should have three yellow loops and one red loop. Have students lay the red loop on their desks in the shape of a circle. Then have them overlap the red circle with the three yellow circles, so the arrangement now looks like this:

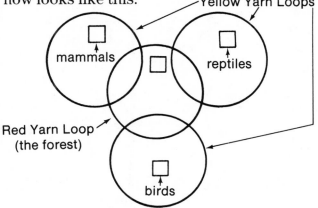

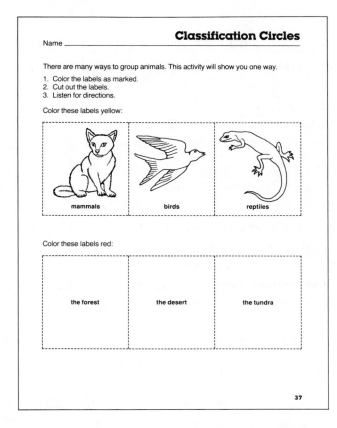

The red label *the forest* should be put inside the red loop, and the three yellow labels, *mammals*, *birds*, and *reptiles* should be placed inside the yellow circles. Make sure the students put the yellow labels outside the intersection points of the yellow and red loops.

3. Have students group the animal cards from page 38 by type (mammal, bird, or reptile). Then have them put the cards in the appropriate yellow circles. Ask students to find the animals in each circle that live in the forest. Have them move these cards to the intersection spaces between the yellow and red loops. When they have finished the exercise you might have them explain why we would want to organize the cards in this fashion.

4. Repeat the process using one of the other red labels.

Discovery Questions

- How are the desert and the tundra similar?
- How are the desert and the tundra different?

What's an Arthropod?

Concepts

Arthropods are invertebrates with jointed legs and outer skeletons. Three types of arthropods are insects, arachnids, and crustaceans.

Process Emphasis

Grouping

Materials

For each student:
- Activity worksheet, page 39
- Pen or pencil

For the class:
- Pictures of different insects, arachnids (spiders), and crustaceans

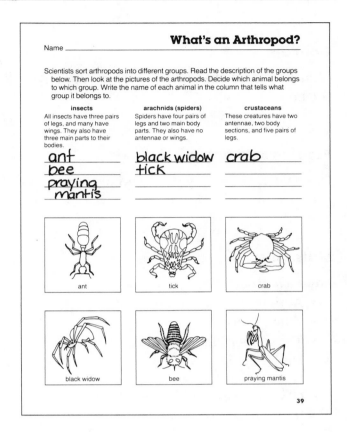

Procedure

1. Lead students into a discussion about arthropods. Point out that these creatures do not have bones inside their bodies. Instead, they have a hard outside covering called an exoskeleton. Arthropods also have many pairs of legs that are covered by the exoskeleton. The legs can only bend at the joints of the exoskeleton. Show students the pictures. Point out the exoskeleton and the jointed legs. Explain that there are different types of arthropods. Some of these are insects, some are arachnids (spiders), and some are crustaceans. Discuss the differences between these groups.

2. Hand out the worksheet. Have students read the description of each group of arthropod. They should write the names of the creatures in each group in the appropriate blanks.

Discovery Questions

- What type of arthropod is a butterfly?

Sensitive Sensors

Concept

Skin receptors are unevenly distributed over the body.

Process Emphasis

Observing, collecting data, and drawing conclusions

Materials

For each student:
- Activity worksheet, page 40
- Fine-point pen
- Two paper clips
- Dull pencil
- Glass of ice water
- Glass of very hot water
- Ruler

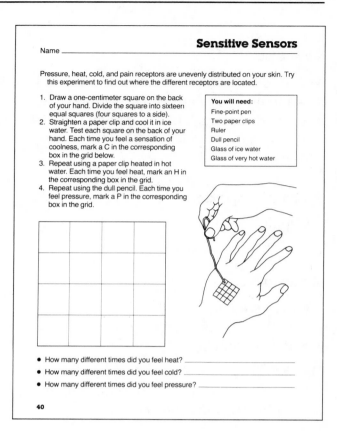

Name _____

Sensitive Sensors

Pressure, heat, cold, and pain receptors are unevenly distributed on your skin. Try this experiment to find out where the different receptors are located.

1. Draw a one-centimeter square on the back of your hand. Divide the square into sixteen equal squares (four squares to a side).
2. Straighten a paper clip and cool it in ice water. Test each square on the back of your hand. Each time you feel a sensation of coolness, mark a C in the corresponding box in the grid below.
3. Repeat using a paper clip heated in hot water. Each time you feel heat, mark an H in the corresponding box in the grid.
4. Repeat using the dull pencil. Each time you feel pressure, mark a P in the corresponding box in the grid.

You will need:
Fine-point pen
Two paper clips
Ruler
Dull pencil
Glass of ice water
Glass of very hot water

- How many different times did you feel heat? _____
- How many different times did you feel cold? _____
- How many different times did you feel pressure? _____

40

Procedure

1. Ask students to close their eyes and touch the surface of their desks, their sleeves, and their pencils. Then have them open their eyes and discuss what they felt. Explain that we can pick up information because we have sense receptors. Discuss the skin receptors for pressure, cold, heat, and pain. Point out that these receptors are located at different points and different depths within the skin.

2. Hand out the worksheet and the materials. Lead students through the directions on the worksheet. (Some students may have problems drawing the small square on the back of their hands—you might have to help them with this.) When students have finished the experiment, they should answer the questions at the bottom of the page.

Discovery Questions

- Is your grid different from the grids of your classmates? If so, why do you think this is?

Mapping Your Tongue

Concept

The taste buds for the four basic tastes are located in different areas of the tongue.

Process Emphasis

Observing, collecting data, and organizing data

Materials

For each student:
- Activity worksheet, page 41
- Four flat toothpicks
- Four small paper cups
- Cup of drinking water

For the class:
- Saltwater
- Sugar water
- Vinegar
- Prepared black tea

Procedure

1. Have students volunteer the names of various foods. Discuss the taste of each food. Explain that there are four basic tastes that most people recognize. Discuss taste buds and how they allow us to taste food.

2. Have the students put a small amount of each liquid into a separate cup. Ask the students to dip a toothpick into the first cup and touch it to different areas of their tongues. Each time the student can taste the liquid he or she should make a mark on the tongue map (on the worksheet). Have students repeat this process for the remaining liquids. Make sure they rinse out their mouths before tasting the next liquid.

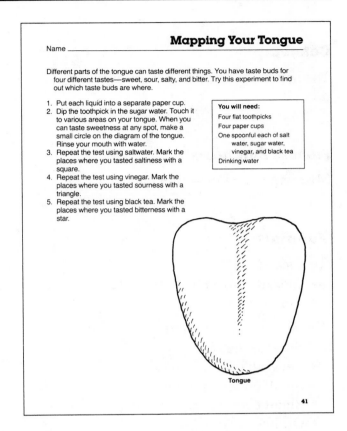

Mapping Your Tongue

Name _____

Different parts of the tongue can taste different things. You have taste buds for four different tastes—sweet, sour, salty, and bitter. Try this experiment to find out which taste buds are where.

1. Put each liquid into a separate paper cup.
2. Dip the toothpick in the sugar water. Touch it to various areas on your tongue. When you can taste sweetness at any spot, make a small circle on the diagram of the tongue. Rinse your mouth with water.
3. Repeat the test using saltwater. Mark the places where you tasted saltiness with a square.
4. Repeat the test using vinegar. Mark the places where you tasted sourness with a triangle.
5. Repeat the test using black tea. Mark the places where you tasted bitterness with a star.

You will need:
Four flat toothpicks
Four paper cups
One spoonful each of salt water, sugar water, vinegar, and black tea
Drinking water

Tongue

41

Discovery Questions

- If we only have four basic tastes, why do different foods have distinctly different tastes?
- Why can't you taste things as well when you have a cold?

Tasty Smells

Concept

The senses of smell and taste are closely related.

Process Emphasis

Observing and collecting data

Materials

For each student:
- Activity worksheet, page 42
- Pen or pencil

For each pair of students:
- Several mint leaves
- Several lettuce leaves
- Small cubes of apple
- Small cubes of raw potato
- Orange segments
- Lemon segments

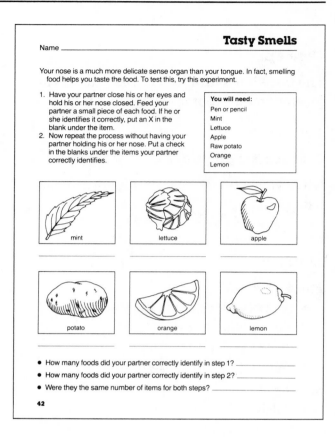

Procedure

1. Divide the class into groups of two. Hand out the worksheet and foods. Lead the students through the directions on the worksheet.

2. Discuss the olfactory nerve and how it carries "smell" messages from the nose to the brain. Also explain that when we eat, smell information and taste information travels to the brain. The brain receives the smell messages before the taste messages. Often, you are smelling food when you think you are tasting it. This is why food seems tasteless when the passages in your nose are closed off.

Discovery Questions

- How might our sense of smell be a safety device for our bodies?
- Why do you know how food tastes before you chew it?

Tracking Human Traits

Concept

Variations of human traits can be seen among people. The traits are controlled by dominant and recessive genes.

Process Emphasis

Observing, collecting data, and drawing conclusions

Materials

For each student:
- Activity worksheet, page 43
- Pen or pencil

Procedure

1. Discuss dominant and recessive traits in humans, such as height limit, freckles, and hair color. Point out that most traits express themselves through the interaction of dominant and recessive genes. You might also want to explain that dominant does not mean better, and recessive does not mean worse.

2. Hand out the worksheet. Lead students through the directions. Divide the class into pairs and have each pair complete the first three questions on the worksheet. When everyone is finished, have the students tabulate the results for the class on the chalkboard. They should copy this information into the chart on their worksheet and answer the questions at the bottom of the page.

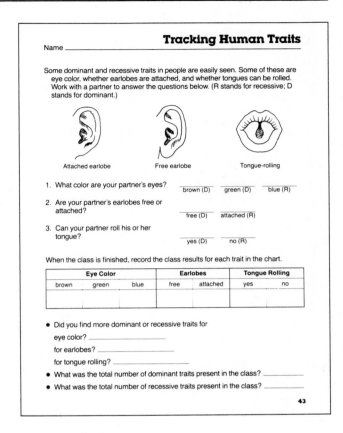

Discovery Questions

- Can you find dominant and recessive traits in plants? If so, what are some examples?
- Can you find dominant and recessive traits in animals? If so, what are some examples?

ACTIVITY WORKSHEETS

Name _____

Identify the flowering plants below. Examine the pictures and decide whether each plant is a monocot or a dicot. Write *monocot* or *dicot* on the line under each plant. (Hint: Count the number of petals and look at the vein patterns in the leaves.)

lily of the valley

_____

petunia

_____

round-leafed violet

_____

daisy

_____

daffodil

_____

California poppy

_____

orchid

_____

geranium

_____

Adventures in Life Science, © 1987 David S. Lake Publishers

Dissect a Flower!

Name _____

1. Spread newspaper on your desk and place the flower on it.

2. Draw the flower in the box below. Show and label all the parts you can see.

3. Examine and count the petals. Remove the petals.

   How many petals are there? _____

   What color are the petals? _____

4. Remove a stamen. Look at the end with the hand lens.

   What do you see? _____

5. Touch the end of the pistil. Then rub a stamen on the pistil. Look at the pistil through the lens.

   What does the pistil feel like? _____

   What happens when you rub the stamen on the pistil? _____

6. Locate the ovary. Split the ovary open with your fingernail.

   Are there eggs inside? If so, how many? _____

Adventures in Life Science, © 1987 David S. Lake Publishers

Name _____

1. Measure the length of each peanut shell to the nearest millimeter, and record each length in the chart.

2. Complete the graph. Show how many peanuts you have of each length by coloring the correct number of squares.

You will need:

ten peanuts in the shell

centimeter ruler

pencil

Peanut	1	2	3	4	5	6	7	8	9	10
Length (cm)										

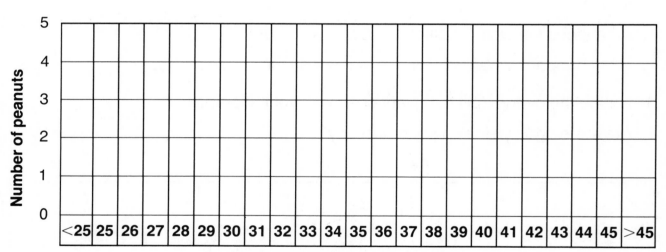

Length of peanut in millimeters

- What is the range from the shortest length to the longest length? _____

- What is the average length? (To find the average length, add all the length measurements. Divide this number by ten.)

_____

- How many peanuts are the same length as the average length?

_____

Adventures in Life Science, © 1987 David S. Lake Publishers

Hitchhikers, Floaters, and Flyers

Name _____

In order for plants to grow well, the seeds must be scattered. Different seeds scatter in different ways.

Test each seed, using the tests below. Read the descriptions to determine which type of seed it is. Then paste the seed in a box that shows what type it is.

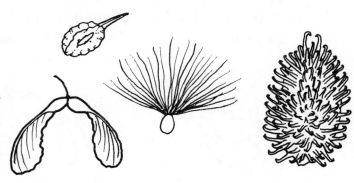

Tests

1. Try blowing a seed from your hand.

2. Try floating the seed on the water.

3. Try touching the cloth lightly to the seed.

Descriptions

Flyers: These seeds can be carried by wind.

Floaters: These seeds can float on water.

Hitchhikers: These seeds will stick on cloth, fur, and feathers.

Flyers					
Floaters					
Hitchhikers					

Name _____

If you look at a lot of different leaves, you will notice the leaves have different types of edges. Use the samples below to name the edge pattern for each leaf. Write *smooth, toothed*, or *lobed* on the blank under each leaf.

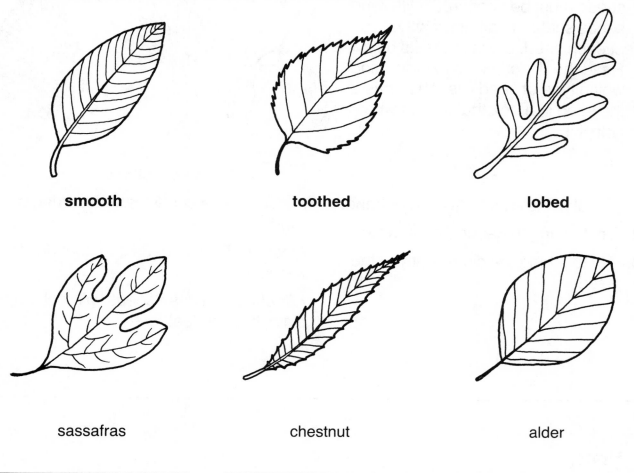

smooth   **toothed**   **lobed**

sassafras   chestnut   alder

_____   _____   _____

live oak   California oak   willow

_____   _____   _____

The Edible Parts

Can you identify the different plant parts we eat? Pretend you are on a food scavenger hunt. Name as many edible plants as you can that fit into the categories below. Write the names in the appropriate columns. Some samples have already been done for you.

roots	stems	leaves	flowers	ovaries or fruit	seeds
carrots	celery	parsley thyme	broccoli	peaches tomatoes	nuts

Do Plants Breathe?

Is heat one of the products of plant respiration? Try this experiment to find out.

1. Moisten the cotton balls with water (the cotton should not be soaking wet). Cover the bottom of each jar with the cotton balls.
2. Place the bean seeds in one jar and the boiled bean seeds in the other.
3. Cover the top of each jar with a piece of paper. Use rubber bands to keep the paper in place.
4. Punch a small hole in the paper using a pencil. Stick one thermometer through the hole. Make sure the thermometer is touching the beans.
5. Check the temperature of each jar every day for a week. (You should check it at the same time each day.) Record the temperatures in the chart below.
6. At the end of the week, answer the questions.

You will need:

Two thick glass jars
Two thermometers
Two rubber bands
Paper
Cotton balls
Water
Bean sprout seeds
Boiled bean sprout seeds
Pen or pencil

	Temperature (°)				
	Day 1	Day 2	Day 3	Day 4	Day 5
Live bean seeds					
Boiled bean seeds					

● Did one jar have a higher temperature than the other? If so, which one? _____

● Why did you test both live bean seeds and dead bean seeds?

_____

Adventures in Life Science, © 1987 David S. Lake Publishers

Populations by a Pond

Name _____

Use the following information to fill in the bar graph below. Use a different color for each population.

- There are six types of populations in this area.
- There are 20 ducks.
- There are 80 lily pads.
- There are 25 bullfrogs.
- There are 110 mosquitoes.
- There are 50 minnows.
- There are 15 snails.

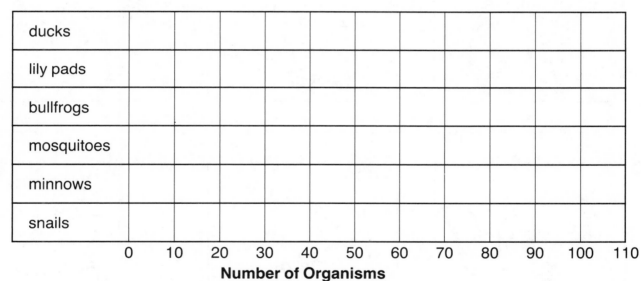

Use the information to answer the following questions.

1. Which population is the largest? _____

2. Which population is the smallest? _____

3. What do you think would happen to the size of the frog population if all the

   mosquitoes disappeared? _____

4. What do you think would happen to the size of the duck population if there

   were twice as many fish? _____

Name _____

The plants and animals on this page belong either to a forest community or to a pond community. Write the community that each organism belongs to under its picture.

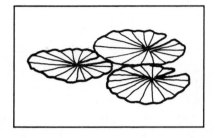

_____

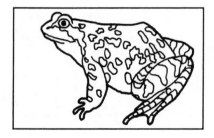

_____

_____

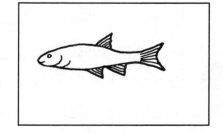

_____

Food Chains

Name _____

Each column represents a food chain. Put the pictures in order by numbering each picture. Use the number 1 for the lowest organism on the chain.

Food Chain A   **Food Chain B**

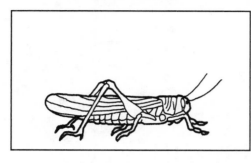

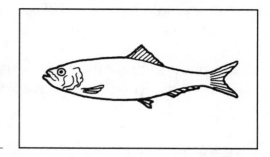

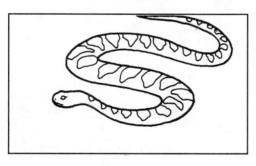

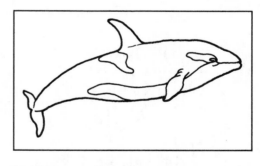

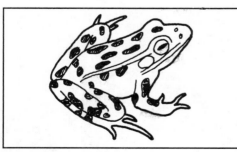

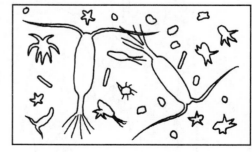

- Where would you find Food Chain A? _____
- Where would you find Food Chain B? _____

Survival Specialists

Many animals have special body parts that help them survive in their environments. Read the descriptions of the animals. Next to each picture, write the letter of the correct description of the animal.

A. This animal uses its handlike paws to catch fish and frogs.

B. The pointed beak on this animal allows it to dig under tree bark for insects.

C. This animal uses echos to find and eat insects in the air.

D. The long, curved claws of this animal allow it to dig tunnels to look for rodents.

E. This animal uses its sharp teeth to crack nuts.

1. _____

2. _____

3. _____

4. _____

5. _____

Adventures in Life Science, © 1987 David S. Lake Publishers

Camouflage It!

Each of the animals on this page uses camouflage to defend itself from enemies. Look at each animal and the two scenes next to it. Circle the scene in which the animal's camouflage will work best. Describe the reason for your choice on the lines provided.

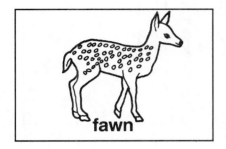 

_____
_____
_____

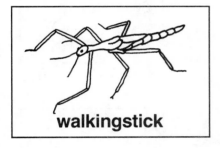 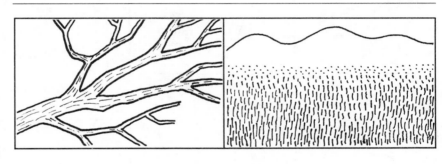

_____
_____
_____

 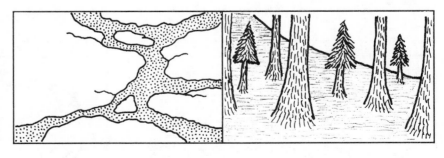

_____
_____
_____

What's the Difference?

Name _____

All of the animals on this page are vertebrates (animals with backbones). In each row, circle the animal that does not belong with the rest. Then explain the reason for your choice on the line.

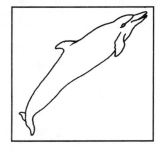   

Classification Circles

Name _____

There are many ways to group animals. This activity will show you one way.

1. Color the labels as marked.
2. Cut out the labels.
3. Listen for directions.

Color these labels yellow:

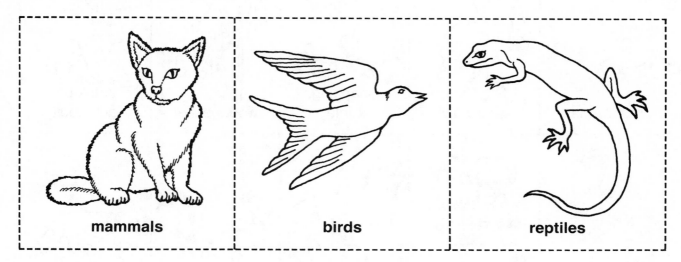

mammals   **birds**   **reptiles**

Color these labels red:

the forest   **the desert**   **the tundra**

Classification Circles

You will use these cards with the labels on page 37.

1. Cut out the cards.
2. Listen for directions.

roadrunner	snowy owl	snapping turtle	woodpecker	antelope jackrabbit
cedar waxwing	garter snake	coyote	gray squirrel	arctic fox
white-tailed deer	sidewinder	racoon	musk ox	salamander
caribou	iguana	gila monster	cactus wren	arctic loon

Adventures in Life Science, © 1987 David S. Lake Publishers

What's an Arthropod?

Scientists sort arthropods into different groups. Read the description of the groups below. Then look at the pictures of the arthropods. Decide which animal belongs to which group. Write the name of each animal in the column that tells what group it belongs to.

insects

All insects have three pairs of legs, and many have wings. They also have three main parts to their bodies.

arachnids (spiders)

Spiders have four pairs of legs and two main body parts. They also have no antennae or wings.

crustaceans

These creatures have two antennae, two body sections, and five pairs of legs.

_____   _____   _____

_____   _____   _____

_____   _____   _____

_____   _____   _____

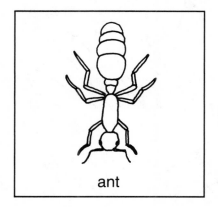

ant

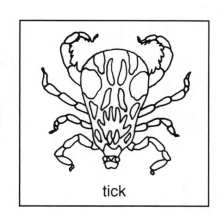

tick

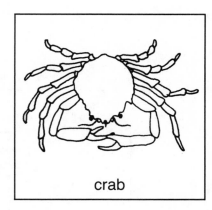

crab

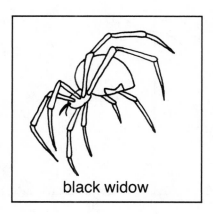

black widow

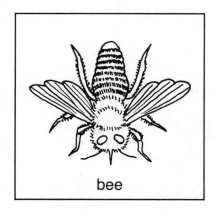

bee

praying mantis

Sensitive Sensors

Name _____

Pressure, heat, cold, and pain receptors are unevenly distributed on your skin. Try this experiment to find out where the different receptors are located.

1. Draw a one-centimeter square on the back of your hand. Divide the square into sixteen equal squares (four squares to a side).
2. Straighten a paper clip and cool it in ice water. Test each square on the back of your hand. Each time you feel a sensation of coolness, mark a C in the corresponding box in the grid below.
3. Repeat using a paper clip heated in hot water. Each time you feel heat, mark an H in the corresponding box in the grid.
4. Repeat using the dull pencil. Each time you feel pressure, mark a P in the corresponding box in the grid.

You will need:

Fine-point pen

Two paper clips

Ruler

Dull pencil

Glass of ice water

Glass of very hot water

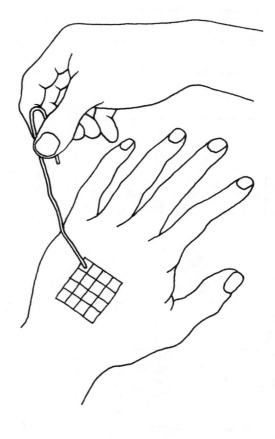

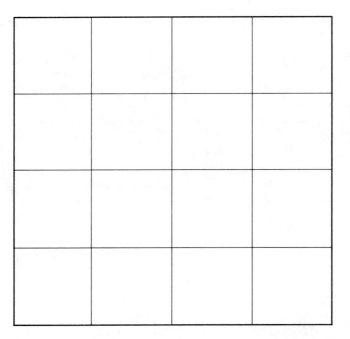

- How many different times did you feel heat? _____
- How many different times did you feel cold? _____
- How many different times did you feel pressure? _____

Adventures in Life Science, © 1987 David S. Lake Publishers

Mapping Your Tongue

Name _____

Different parts of the tongue can taste different things. You have taste buds for four different tastes—sweet, sour, salty, and bitter. Try this experiment to find out which taste buds are where.

1. Put each liquid into a separate paper cup.
2. Dip the toothpick in the sugar water. Touch it to various areas on your tongue. When you can taste sweetness at any spot, make a small circle on the diagram of the tongue. Rinse your mouth with water.
3. Repeat the test using saltwater. Mark the places where you tasted saltiness with a square.
4. Repeat the test using vinegar. Mark the places where you tasted sourness with a triangle.
5. Repeat the test using black tea. Mark the places where you tasted bitterness with a star.

> **You will need:**
>
> Four flat toothpicks
>
> Four paper cups
>
> One spoonful each of salt water, sugar water, vinegar, and black tea
>
> Drinking water

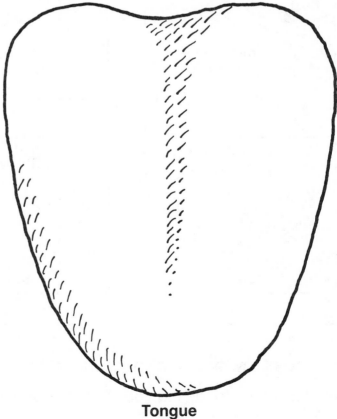

Tongue

Adventures in Life Science. © 1987 David S. Lake Publishers

Tasty Smells

Your nose is a much more delicate sense organ than your tongue. In fact, smelling food helps you taste the food. To test this, try this experiment.

1. Have your partner close his or her eyes and hold his or her nose closed. Feed your partner a small piece of each food. If he or she identifies it correctly, put an X in the blank under the item.
2. Now repeat the process without having your partner holding his or her nose. Put a check in the blanks under the items your partner correctly identifies.

You will need:

Pen or pencil

Mint

Lettuce

Apple

Raw potato

Orange

Lemon

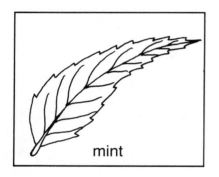

mint

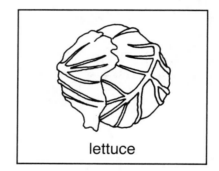

lettuce

apple

_____

_____

_____

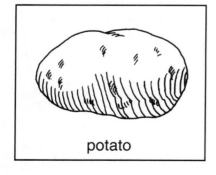

potato

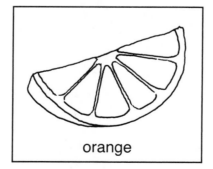

orange

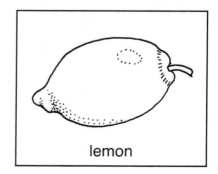

lemon

_____

_____

_____

- How many foods did your partner correctly identify in step 1? _____
- How many foods did your partner correctly identify in step 2? _____
- Were they the same number of items for both steps? _____

Adventures in Life Science, © 1987 David S. Lake Publishers

Tracking Human Traits

Name _____

Some dominant and recessive traits in people are easily seen. Some of these are eye color, whether earlobes are attached, and whether tongues can be rolled. Work with a partner to answer the questions below. (R stands for recessive; D stands for dominant.)

Attached earlobe

Free earlobe

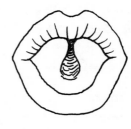

Tongue-rolling

1. What color are your partner's eyes?

    _____ _____ _____
    brown (D)   green (D)   blue (R)

2. Are your partner's earlobes free or attached?

    _____ _____
    free (D)   attached (R)

3. Can your partner roll his or her tongue?

    _____ _____
    yes (D)   no (R)

When the class is finished, record the class results for each trait in the chart.

Eye Color			Earlobes		Tongue Rolling	
brown	green	blue	free	attached	yes	no

- Did you find more dominant or recessive traits for

    eye color? _____

    for earlobes? _____

    for tongue rolling? _____

- What was the total number of dominant traits present in the class? _____

- What was the total number of recessive traits present in the class? _____

Doing Science

Adventures in Earth Science

Process-Oriented Activities for Grades 4–6

PART 5   ADVENTURES IN EARTH SCIENCE

CONTENTS

TEACHER'S GUIDE

Future Forecasts

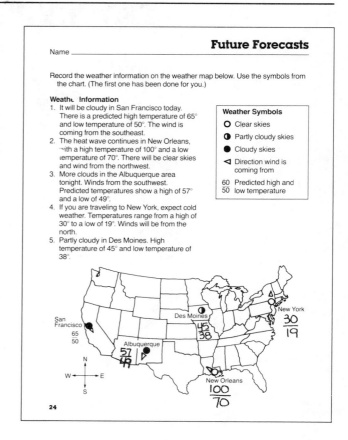

Concept

Weather maps are useful sources of information.

Process Emphasis

Organizing data

Materials

For each student:
- Activity worksheet, page 24
- Pen or pencil

For the class:
- Weather maps from a local paper

Procedure

1. Ask students to suggest types of information that should be included in a weather report. Be open to suggestions such as wind speed and direction, location of storm fronts, temperatures, and precipitation. Show students the weather maps. Explain that these maps show weather predictions for the area. Discuss the symbols on the maps. (Note: different areas use different symbols.)

2. Hand out the worksheet. Ask students to read the weather information and record it on the map. Ask them to use the symbols listed on the page. You might also have them record that day's prediction on their maps.

Discovery Questions

- What do you think a hurricane would look like on a weather map?
- What are some of the instruments people use to get information about weather?

Under Pressure

Concept

Barometers measure the air pressure and help us predict the weather.

Process Emphasis

Measuring and collecting data

Materials

For each student:
- Activity worksheet, page 25
- Pencil

For each group of four students:
- Large baby-food jar
- Scissors
- Balloon
- Paper or plastic straw
- Rubber bands
- White glue
- Cardboard
- Ruler

Procedure

1. Explain that a *barometer* measures air pressure. The needle on a barometer moves as the air pressure changes. Divide the class into groups of four. Hand out the materials and lead the class through the directions on the worksheet. Have students measure the barometric pressure twice a day, at the same times each day. They should also observe the weather changes during the week.

2. At the end of the week, have students compare their barometric changes with the weather. Ask them to look for patterns, such as high readings bring clear weather and low readings precede storms.

Discovery Questions

- How could your barometer help you predict the weather?
- What is the difference between an aneroid barometer and a mercury barometer?

Under Pressure

Name _____

The pressure of the air can be measured using a barometer. In this activity you will build your own barometer. It will give you a general idea of how air pressure relates to weather conditions.

1. Cut a large section from the balloon and stretch it tightly over the mouth of the jar. Have someone place a rubber band or two around the balloon section so it will stay in place.
2. Cut the end of the straw so that it forms a point.
3. Put a drop of glue in the center of the balloon section. Place the nonpointed end of the straw lengthwise on the spot of glue. Hold the straw until it is set.
4. Fold the cardboard until it can stand by itself. Place it next to the pointed end of the straw and mark a line on the cardboard where the straw points. Label the mark with the number 5.
5. Make five marks counting up and five marks down from the 5. The marks should be 3 millimeters apart. Write the numbers 0 through 10 at the marks.
6. Realign with the straw next to the number 5. Check your barometer twice a day for a week. Record the barometric reading in the chart below. You should also record whether the barometer is rising or falling and the weather conditions for each day.

You will need:
large baby-food jar
scissors
balloon
paper or plastic straw
rubber bands
white glue
cardboard
ruler
pencil

	A.M.	P.M.	Rising or Falling?	Weather Conditions
Monday				
Tuesday				
Wednesday				
Thursday				
Friday				

25

Hot Enough for You?

Concept

Sunlight affects air temperature.

Process Emphasis

Measuring, collecting data, and organizing data

Materials

For each student:
- Activity worksheet, page 26
- Colored pencils

For the class:
- Three thermometers

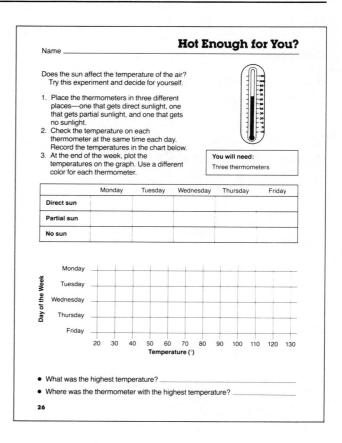

Procedure

1. Have students place the thermometers in three different places—one that gets direct sunlight, one that gets partial sunlight, and one that gets no sunlight. (Note: if you are doing this activity during the early fall or late spring, make sure your thermometers can handle very high temperatures.) Have students check the thermometers once a day for a week. They should check the temperatures at the same time each day and record their findings on the worksheet. At the end of the week, have students plot their findings on the graph provided. You may have to remind them how to plot information on graphs. Ask them to discuss their findings.

Discovery Questions

- What is the hottest place on earth?
- What is the coldest place on earth?
- What are some other factors besides sunlight that influence air temperature?

Blowing in the Wind

Concept

Wind speed can be observed.

Process Emphasis

Comparing and collecting data

Materials

For each student:
- Activity worksheet, page 27
- Pen or pencil

Blowing in the Wind

Name _____

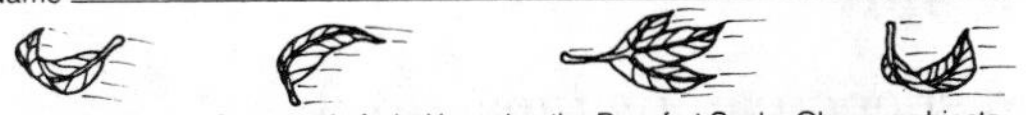

You can estimate the speed of wind by using the Beaufort Scale. Observe objects outside once a day at the same time each day. Record your observations in the chart below. Then use the Beaufort Scale to find the name and speed of the wind. Write the information in the chart.

Beaufort Scale of Wind Speeds

Observation	Name of Wind	Miles per Hour
Smoke goes straight up	Calm	Less than 1
Smoke moves but weather vanes do not	Light Air	1–3
Weather vanes move; leaves rustle	Light Breeze	4–7
Flags flutter; leaves move constantly	Gentle Breeze	8–12
Dirt and paper raised; flags flap	Moderate Breeze	13–18
Small trees sway; flags ripple	Fresh Breeze	19–24
Large branches move; flags beat	Strong Breeze	25–31
Whole trees sway; flags are extended	Moderate Gale	32–38
Twigs break off; hard to walk against	Fresh Gale	39–46
Slight damage to buildings	Strong Gale	47–54
Trees uprooted; windows break	Full Gale	55–63
Widespread damage to buildings	Violent Storm	64–75
General destruction	Hurricane	Over 75

	Observations	Name of wind	Miles per hour
Monday			
Tuesday			
Wednesday			
Thursday			
Friday			

- Which day had the fastest wind? What was the wind speed? _____
- Which day had the slowest wind? What was the wind speed? _____

27

Procedure

1. Ask students to point out evidence that the air is moving (tree branches and grass bending, hair blowing, whistling sounds). Then ask them if they can think of a way to measure the speed of the wind without using any instruments. Explain that they could observe the motions of various objects such as flags, leaves, and chimney smoke to get an idea of how strong the wind is. Discuss the Beaufort Scale shown on the worksheet.

2. Hand out the worksheet. Have students observe the wind once a day for a week. (Measurements should be made at the same time each day.) Explain that they should record their observations and use the Beaufort Scale to determine the name and the strength of the wind.

Discovery Questions

- Which wind is stronger—a hurricane or a tornado?
- Which allows you to see very slight air movement—chimney smoke or large tree branches?
- Which allows you to see very strong air movement—chimney smoke or trees?

The Windy Cities

Concept

Wind speed can be measured.

Process Emphasis

Comparing and grouping

Materials

For each student:
- Activity worksheet, page 28
- Pen or pencil

Procedure

1. Ask students if they can think of a way to measure the wind. Draw a picture of an anemometer on the board or for an overhead projector (see Figure A). Explain that scientists measure wind speed with a device called an *anemometer*. Ask students if they can tell you how the anemometer works. (Cups on the device turn when wind hits them. The faster the wind, the faster the cups turn. The cups are connected to a dial that shows the wind speed.) Discuss their answers.

2. Hand out the worksheet. Explain that on weather maps, certain symbols are used to indicate wind speed. Discuss the symbols shown on the worksheet. Have students identify the wind speed for each city and write the names of the cities in the proper columns.

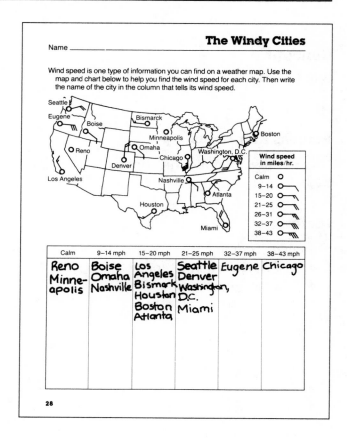

Discovery Questions

- How is wind created?
- Does the wind always come from the same direction?

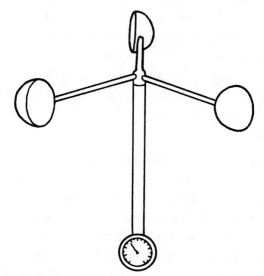

Figure A: anemometer

Here Today, Gone Tomorrow

Concept

Wind, water, and ice erosion change the shape of the land.

Process Emphasis

Sequencing

Materials

For each student:
- Activity worksheet, page 29
- Pen or pencil

For the class:
- A pile of dry sand
- A rectangular cake pan
- Ice cubes
- Large pitcher of water

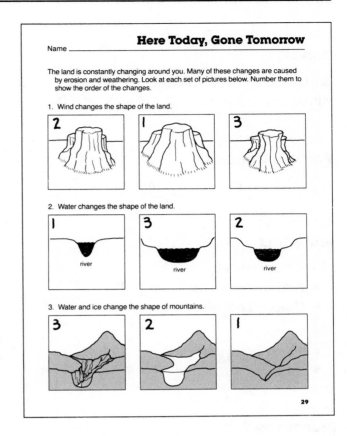

Procedure

1. Demonstrate the effects of erosion in the following ways:

Wind Erosion: Pile the sand in the cake pan. Ask students what they think will happen if you blow on the sand. Blow on the sand. Have students observe and discuss the effects.

Ice Erosion: Pile wet sand in the cake pan. Ask students what they think will happen if you put ice cubes (to represent a glacier) on top of the sand mountain. Place the ice on top of the sand. Have students observe and discuss the effects.

Water Erosion: Pile wet sand in the cake pan. Make a narrow downhill trench in the sand to indicate a river's path. Ask students what they think will happen when water rushes through the sand. Pour a steady stream of water into the top of the trench. Have students observe and discuss the effects.

2. Hand out the worksheet. Have students number the pictures of erosion to show the order of the events.

Discovery Questions

- What is the difference between erosion and weathering?
- How was the Grand Canyon formed?

Shake, Rattle, and Roll

Concept

Earthquakes are a shaking of the earth caused by movement of rocks along a fault.

Process Emphasis

Organizing data and drawing conclusions

Materials

For each student:
- Activity worksheet, page 30
- Colored pencils

For the class:
- Three colors of clay
- Knife

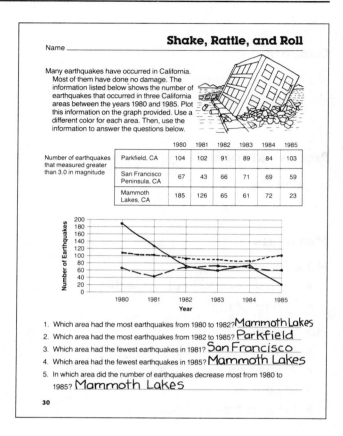

Procedure

1. Flatten the pieces of clay. Tell the students that the clay represents layers of rocks in the earth's crust. Stack and press the layers on top of one another. Push in the sides so the clay folds up (see Figure A). Point out that just as the clay formed folds because of pressure, pressures from inside or outside the earth's crust can force layers of rock to fold up.

2. Explain to the class that a *fault* occurs when a break occurs in the earth's crust. The land can shift up or down along the crack or sideways along the crack. Slice the clay with a knife to separate it. Place the two pieces of clay near each other, but do not align them evenly. Tell the students that this is what a fault looks like. Explain that when huge rocks move along a fault, the ground shakes. This is called an earthquake. Discuss earthquakes and what happens during an earthquake.

3. Hand out the worksheet and pencils. Have the students plot the information on the graph. (You may want to demonstrate this graphing technique.) When the students have finished their graphs, they should answer the questions at the bottom of the page.

Discovery Questions

- What is the Richter Scale?
- Why do earthquakes often happen in California?

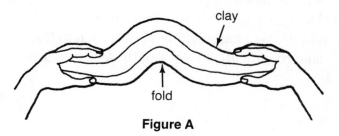

Figure A

Hot Rocks!

Concept

Igneous rocks are formed from hardened magma.

Process Emphasis

Classifying

Materials

For each student:
- Activity worksheet, page 31
- Pen or pencil
- Crayons or colored pencils (optional)

For the class:
- Samples of igneous rocks—granite, basalt, obsidian, and pumice
- Hand lenses (optional)

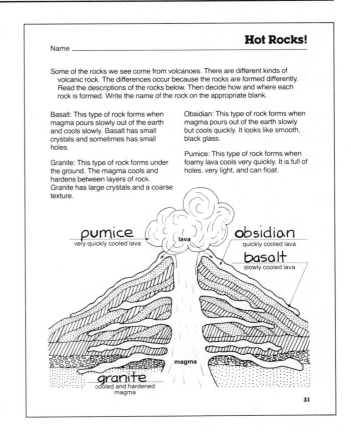

Procedure

1. Show students the rock samples. Explain that these rocks were formed from magma. (You also might want to explain that lava is magma found outside the earth.) Because of this some people call them "fire rocks." You might want to tell students that scientists call the rocks *igneous* rocks, which means rocks from fire. Have students study the samples (you might want to provide hand lenses) and compare their similarities and differences. Point out that the rocks are different because they were formed differently.

2. Hand out the worksheet. Have students write the name of each rock on the proper space. You might also have them color the different parts of the volcano.

Discovery Questions

- Gabbros is a type of rock that forms under the surface of the earth. The magma is slowly cooled and hardened. Does gabbros look more like granite or obsidian?
- Scoria is a rock that is formed by quickly cooled lava. Does scoria look more like granite or pumice?

Don't Take It for Granite!

Concept

Rocks form in different ways.

Process Emphasis

Grouping

Materials

For each student:
- Activity worksheet, page 32
- Pen or pencil

For the class:
- Samples of igneous rocks (granite, pumice, obsidian); sedimentary rocks (limestone, sandstone, chalk, clay); and metamorphic rocks (marble, slate, gneiss). These are usually available at lapidary stores.

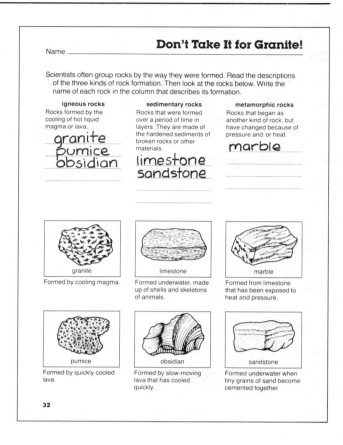

Procedure

1. Show students the rock samples. Have students examine the rocks and describe the characteristics of each rock. Ask them to compare the similarities and the differences of the rocks and see if they can create a way to group them. Explain the different ways in which rocks form. Point out the examples of each form.

2. Hand out the worksheet. Have students read the descriptions of each rock and write the name of the rock in the appropriate blank.

Discovery Questions

- In which type of rock are you most likely to find fossils? Why?
- What can sedimentary rocks tell us about the past?

Scratch and Match

Concept

The minerals in some rocks can be identified by their color.

Process Emphasis

Observing, collecting data, and drawing conclusions

Materials

For each student:
- Activity worksheet, page 33
- Pen or pencil

For each group of four students:
- Piece of unglazed tile
- Four to eight of the following rocks: azurite, chalcopyrite or pyrite, cinnabar, galena*, hematite, limonite, magnetite, malachite or olivine. These are usually available at lapidary stores.

Procedure

1. Divide the class into groups of four. Hand out the materials. Have the students rub one piece of rock at a time across the tile. (This will leave a streak of color on the tile.) Students should record the color of the streak on their worksheets. Have them use the color-sorting key on the page to identify the minerals in each rock.

2. Discuss the activity. Explain that all the rocks in the world are made of minerals—different rocks have different minerals and/ or different amounts of minerals. You might ask students if they can think of other ways to identify the minerals in rocks.

Discovery Questions

- Is the streak test useful if you have several rocks that leave white streaks? Why?
- Why are there differences between the external color of a rock and the color of the streak it leaves?

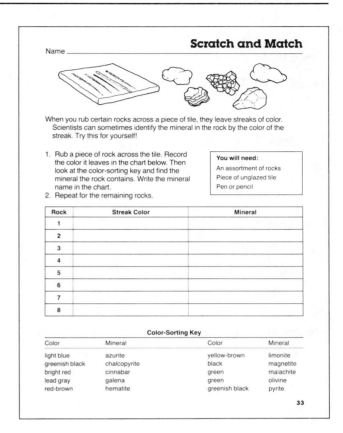

*If you are using galena, make sure students wash their hands thoroughly after handling the material.

Telling Time with Fossils

Concept

Fossils are different ages.

Process Emphasis

Sequencing

Materials

For each student:
- Activity worksheet, page 34
- Pen or pencil

For the class:
- Picture or diagram of sedimentary rock layers

Telling Time with Fossils

Name _____

Scientists can "see back in time" using fossils. Old fossils tell us something about the earth's past. Some fossils are more than two billion years old. Create a fossil time line. Look at the pictures below. Then write the name of each creature under its age on the time line.

Cephalaspis ≈ 410 million years old

Eohippus ≈ 50 million years old

Australopithecus ≈ 2 million years old

Trilobite ≈ 600 million years old

Dimetrodon ≈ 275 million years old

Stegasaurus ≈ 150 million years old

Ichthyostega ≈ 365 million years old

Diatryma ≈ 65 million years old

Millions of years ago

600   500   400   300   200   100   50 0
          410 365   275   150   65

Trilobite   Cephalaspis Ichthyostega   Dimetrodon   Stegasaurus   Diatryma Eohippus Australopithecus

34

Procedure

1. Discuss how sedimentary rock forms. Show students the picture of the rock layers. Explain that scientists find different fossils in the different layers of rock. Since the rock layers build up over time, the oldest layers are on the bottom and the younger layers are on the top. Point out that the oldest fossils are found in the lowest layers of rock. If an outside area is available for digging, you might let students dig in the soil to see if they can detect a difference in layers.

2. Hand out the worksheet. Have students write the name of the organism under its age on the time line.

Discovery Questions

- How are fossils formed?
- How can scientists tell if organisms have changed over time?

Fossil Circles

Concept

Fossils can be classified in many ways.

Process Emphasis

Grouping

Materials

For each student:

- Activity worksheets, pages 35 and 36
- Scissors
- Four pieces 24″ yarn; three yellow and one red

Procedure

1. Duplicate the worksheets on heavy paper and hand out. Have students color the labels on page 35 according to the directions. They should cut out the cards and labels on both pages.

2. Ask students to tie each piece of yarn into a loop. They should have three yellow loops and one red loop. Have students lay the red loop on their desks in the shape of a circle. Then have them overlap the red circle with the three yellow circles, so the arrangement looks like this:

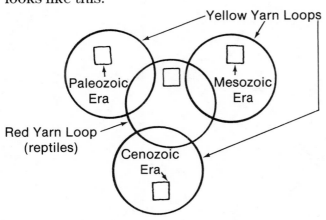

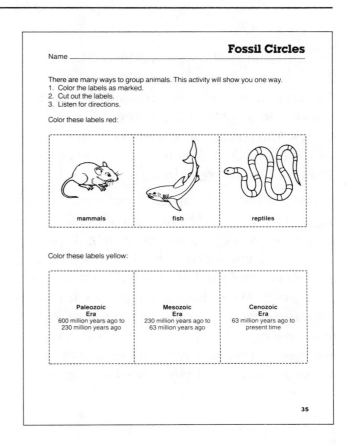

The red label *reptiles* should be put inside the red loop, and the three yellow labels *Paleozoic Era, Mesozoic Era,* and *Cenozoic Era* should be placed inside the yellow circles. Make sure the students put the yellow labels outside the intersection points of the yellow and red circles.

3. Have students group the fossil cards from page 36 by age. (Note: the ages of the fossils are on the cards.) Then have them put the cards in the appropriate yellow circles. Ask students to find the fossils in each circle that are reptiles. Have them move these cards to the intersection spaces between the yellow and red loops. When they have finished the exercise you might have them explain why we would want to organize the cards in this fashion.

4. Repeat the process using one of the other red labels.

Discovery Questions

- To which era do human beings belong?
- Why did the dinosaurs become extinct?

Inside or Out?

Concept

We can group the nine planets of our Solar System into two groups—inner planets (the four planets closest to the sun) and outer planets (the five planets farthest from the sun).

Process Emphasis

Classifying

Materials

For each student:
- Activity worksheet, page 37
- Pen or pencil

For the class:
- Pictures of the nine planets

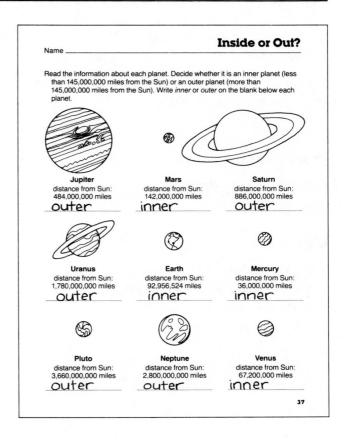

Name _____

Inside or Out?

Read the information about each planet. Decide whether it is an inner planet (less than 145,000,000 miles from the Sun) or an outer planet (more than 145,000,000 miles from the Sun). Write *inner* or *outer* on the blank below each planet.

Jupiter
distance from Sun:
484,000,000 miles
outer

Mars
distance from Sun:
142,000,000 miles
inner

Saturn
distance from Sun:
886,000,000 miles
outer

Uranus
distance from Sun:
1,780,000,000 miles
outer

Earth
distance from Sun:
92,956,524 miles
inner

Mercury
distance from Sun:
36,000,000 miles
inner

Pluto
distance from Sun:
3,660,000,000 miles
outer

Neptune
distance from Sun:
2,800,000,000 miles
outer

Venus
distance from Sun:
67,200,000 miles
inner

37

Procedure

1. Show students the pictures of the planets. Ask them to tell you as much as they can about each planet. Discuss the similarities and differences between the planets. Explain that there are many ways to compare the planets and one way is to compare their distances from the sun.

2. Hand out the worksheet. Have students classify each planet as an inner planet or an outer planet. They should write *inner* or *outer* on the blank below each planet.

Discovery Questions

- What are some of the similarities the four innermost planets share?
- What are some of the similarities the four largest planets share?
- How is Pluto similar to Earth?
- How is Pluto different from Earth?

As the Worlds Turn

Concept

The planets take different amounts of time to circle around the Sun.

Process Emphasis

Comparing and drawing conclusions

Materials

For each student:
- Activity worksheet, page 38
- Pen or pencil

As the Worlds Turn

Name _____

Each planet takes a different amount of time to make a complete circle around the Sun. For example, it takes about 365 days for Earth to circle the Sun. But it takes about 88 days for Mercury to circle the Sun, and 90,700 days for Pluto to circle the Sun. Use the following information to help you answer the questions below.

If you were this many Earth-years old:	You would be this many years old if you lived on:			
Earth	**Mercury**	**Mars**	**Jupiter**	**Uranus**
8	33	4	.6	.08
9	37	4.5	.7	.09
10	41	5	.8	.1
11	42	5.5	.9	.11
12	49	6	1.0	.12

1. If you were 8 Earth-years old, how many Mercury-years old would you be? **33**

2. If you were 10 Earth-years old, how many Uranus-years old would you be? **.1**

3. If you were 12 Earth-years old, how many Mars-years old would you be? **6**

4. If you were 41 Mercury-years old, how many Jupiter-years old would you be? **.8**

5. If you were 1 Jupiter-year old, how many Earth-years old would you be? **12**

6. How many Mars-years old are you? **Answers will vary.**

38

Procedure

1. Discuss the term *revolution*. Explain that it takes about 365 days for Earth to make a complete circle around the Sun. (You might want to demonstrate revolution and rotation by having students act as the Sun and Earth.) Tell students that the other planets in the solar system also revolve around the Sun. However, it takes each planet a different amount of time to do so.

2. Hand out the worksheet. Tell students that the chart on the worksheet shows equivalent number of years. For example, it takes Mercury about 88 days to circle the Sun. Therefore, in the time it takes Earth to revolve around the Sun one time, Mercury has revolved around the Sun about four times. Another way to say this is one Earth year is the same amount of time as four Mercury years. Have students answer the questions on the page using the information from the chart.

Discovery Questions

- If you were eleven years old on Earth, would you be older or younger if you lived on Mercury?
- Why do some planets take longer to revolve around the Sun than others?

Faces of the Moon

Concept

As the moon revolves, we can see different amounts of the lighted surface.

Process Emphasis

Comparing and drawing conclusions

Materials

For each student:
- Activity worksheet, page 39
- Pencil

For the class:
- A dark rubber ball
- Flashlight

Faces of the Moon

Name _____

The pictures below show the positions of the moon over a period of a month. The names of the phases we see on earth are written next to each circle. In each circle, draw what the moon would look like from earth during that phase. (The first two are done for you.)

Part You See — New Moon (invisible) — Waning Crescent — Waxing Crescent — First Quarter — Earth — Third Quarter — Waxing Gibbous — Full Moon — Waning Gibbous

39

Procedure

1. Darken the room. Aim the flashlight beam toward the front of the room. Hold the ball in the light beam and have students observe the patterns of light and dark on the ball from different areas of the room. When all students have had the opportunity to observe the patterns, slowly pass the ball through the light. Point out that the light patterns on the ball are similar to the way the moon looks when you observe it for several weeks. Discuss the phases of the moon and the names of the phases.

2. Hand out the worksheet. Explain that the diagram on the page shows the positions of the moon during a month. Students should draw each phase as we would see it on earth.

Discovery Questions

- Does the motion of the moon have an effect on the earth? If so, what is the effect?
- What did we learn about the moon from the Apollo landings?

Eclipse It!

Concept

Eclipses of the sun and moon depend on the positions and movements of the earth, sun, and moon.

Process Emphasis

Comparing

Materials

For each student:
- Activity worksheet, page 40
- Pen or pencil

For the class:
- Gooseneck lamp without a shade
- Globe of the earth
- Small ball
- Small soda bottle

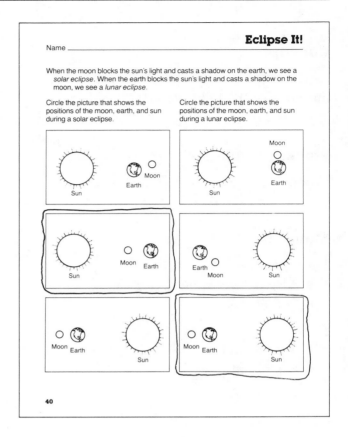

Procedure

1. Ask students if they have ever witnessed a solar or lunar eclipse. Explain that eclipses occur when the earth and moon get in the way of each other's shadows. Demonstrate an eclipse using the lamp as the sun, the globe as the earth, and the small ball as the moon. Place the small ball on the top of the soda bottle and position it between the lamp and the globe so that a shadow of the ball is cast on the globe. Explain that this represents a solar eclipse. Point out that the distance and position of the moon relative to the earth are important. If the moon is too far away from the earth or is to the side of the earth, it will not completely block the sun's light.

2. Hand out the worksheet. Have students compare the drawings and choose the one that shows the proper positions for a lunar eclipse and a solar eclipse.

Discovery Questions

- What is an annular eclipse?
- Could you see solar eclipses if you were on another planet?

The Constellation Game

Concept

People see different patterns in groups of stars.

Process Emphasis

Grouping

Materials

For each student:
- Activity worksheet, page 41
- Pencil

Procedure

1. Explain that years ago people imagined that groups of stars looked like objects or creatures. They would name the groups of stars (constellations) after the creatures or objects they resembled.

2. Hand out the worksheet. Tell students that they should create their own constellations using the groups of stars shown. Have them connect the stars by drawing lines between them. Ask students to name their constellations.

3. When the class is finished, have students display their groupings and compare them with those of their classmates. Point out that different people saw different things in the stars. Explain that this used to happen all the time until a group of people (the

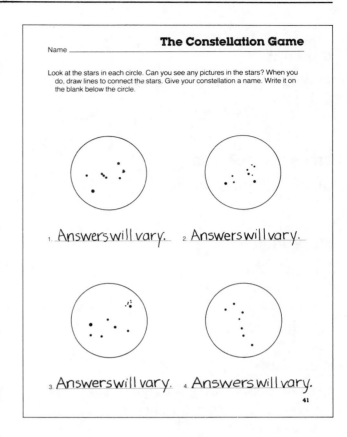

International Astronomical Union) decided on set names for the constellations. Show students the standard names and patterns for the constellations on the worksheet. (1. Orion 2. Leo 3. Taurus 4. Big Dipper)

Discovery Questions

- Why did people see pictures in the stars?
- Are the stars in the constellations really right next to each other?

Starry, Starry Sight

Concept

There are recognizable constellations in the sky.

Process Emphasis

Observing and grouping

Materials

For each student:
- Activity worksheet, page 42
- Pencil

Procedure

1. Draw dots on the chalkboard to represent the stars of the Big Dipper (see Figure A). Ask students if they recognize the pattern on the board. Connect the dots with a solid line to show the pattern. Ask students if this pattern is easier or harder to see once the lines are drawn. Explain that when we look at constellations in the sky we have to imagine the lines between the stars. Sometimes it is easier to find a constellation if you look for a small part of it (for instance, the cup of the Big Dipper).

Figure A: Stars in the Big Dipper

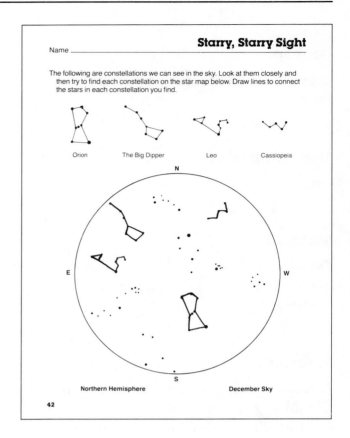

Name _____

Starry, Starry Sight

The following are constellations we can see in the sky. Look at them closely and then try to find each constellation on the star map below. Draw lines to connect the stars in each constellation you find.

Orion   The Big Dipper   Leo   Cassiopeia

Northern Hemisphere   December Sky

42

2. Hand out the worksheet. Have students find the constellations on the star map. Ask them to connect the stars once they have found the constellations.

Discovery Questions

- Would you see the same stars in the sky in January and July? Why?
- Do people in the United States see the same stars as people in England? Why?
- Do people in the United States see the same stars as people in Australia? Why?

How Hot Is Red?

Concept

Stars can be classified by their color and their temperature.

Process Emphasis

Organizing data and drawing conclusions

Materials

For each student:
- Activity worksheet, page 43
- Pencil or colored pencils

For the class:
- Matches, bunsen burner, or candle (optional)

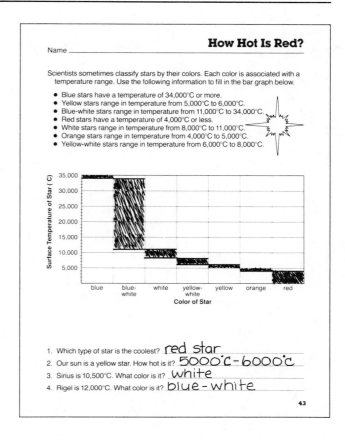

Procedure

1. Ask students what color stars are. (Most students will probably say stars are white.) Explain that stars are actually different colors—blue, white, yellow, orange, or red. Discuss the fact that stars differ in color because they have different surface temperatures. You might want to demonstrate that color is related to temperature using matches, a bunsen burner, or a candle. (If you have the materials, heating a piece of iron will show the range of color from red, cool, to blue-white, very hot.)

2. Hand out the worksheet. Explain to students that they will be graphing *ranges* of temperature. You may want to demonstrate this graphing technique. When the students have finished their graphs, they should answer the questions at the bottom of the page.

Discovery Questions

- Why are stars hot?
- Is the temperature of the inside of a star different from the temperature on the surface of a star? If so, why?

ACTIVITY WORKSHEETS

Future Forecasts

Name _____

Record the weather information on the weather map below. Use the symbols from the chart. (The first one has been done for you.)

Weather Information

1. It will be cloudy in San Francisco today. There is a predicted high temperature of 65° and low temperature of 50°. The wind is coming from the southeast.
2. The heat wave continues in New Orleans, with a high temperature of 100° and a low temperature of 70°. There will be clear skies and wind from the northwest.
3. More clouds in the Albuquerque area tonight. Winds from the southwest. Predicted temperatures show a high of 57° and a low of 49°.
4. If you are traveling to New York, expect cold weather. Temperatures range from a high of 30° to a low of 19°. Winds will be from the north.
5. Partly cloudy in Des Moines. High temperature of 45° and low temperature of 38°.

Weather Symbols

O Clear skies

◑ Partly cloudy skies

● Cloudy skies

◁ Direction wind is coming from

$\frac{60}{50}$ Predicted high and low temperature

Under Pressure

Name _____

The pressure of the air can be measured using a barometer. In this activity you will build your own barometer. It will give you a general idea of how air pressure relates to weather conditions.

1. Cut a large section from the balloon and stretch it tightly over the mouth of the jar. Have someone place a rubber band or two around the balloon section so it will stay in place.
2. Cut the end of the straw so that it forms a point.
3. Put a drop of glue in the center of the balloon section. Place the nonpointed end of the straw lengthwise on the spot of glue. Hold the straw until it is set.
4. Fold the cardboard until it can stand by itself. Place it next to the pointed end of the straw and mark a line on the cardboard where the straw points. Label the mark with the number 5.
5. Make five marks counting up and five marks down from the 5. The marks should be 3 millimeters apart. Write the numbers 0 through 10 at the marks.
6. Realign with the straw next to the number 5. Check your barometer twice a day for a week. Record the barometric reading in the chart below. You should also record whether the barometer is rising or falling and the weather conditions for each day.

You will need:

large baby-food jar
scissors
balloon
paper or plastic straw
rubber bands
white glue
cardboard
ruler
pencil

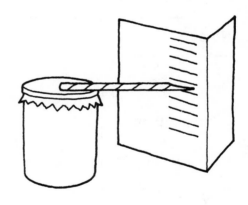

	A.M.	**P.M.**	**Rising or Falling?**	**Weather Conditions**
Monday				
Tuesday				
Wednesday				
Thursday				
Friday				

Hot Enough for You?

Name _____

Does the sun affect the temperature of the air? Try this experiment and decide for yourself.

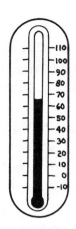

1. Place the thermometers in three different places—one that gets direct sunlight, one that gets partial sunlight, and one that gets no sunlight.
2. Check the temperature on each thermometer at the same time each day. Record the temperatures in the chart below.
3. At the end of the week, plot the temperatures on the graph. Use a different color for each thermometer.

You will need:

Three thermometers

	Monday	Tuesday	Wednesday	Thursday	Friday
Direct sun					
Partial sun					
No sun					

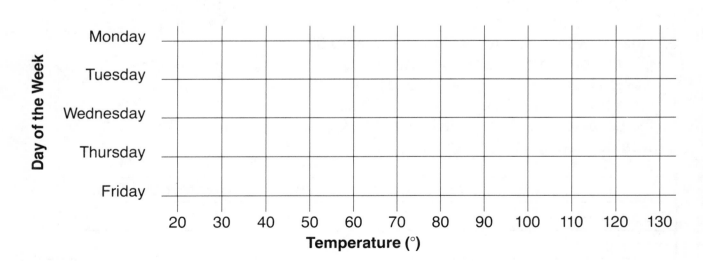

- What was the highest temperature? _____
- Where was the thermometer with the highest temperature? _____

Adventures in Earth Science, © 1987 David S. Lake Publishers

Blowing in the Wind

Name _____

You can estimate the speed of wind by using the Beaufort Scale. Observe objects outside once a day at the same time each day. Record your observations in the chart below. Then use the Beaufort Scale to find the name and speed of the wind. Write the information in the chart.

Beaufort Scale of Wind Speeds		
Observation	**Name of Wind**	**Miles per Hour**
Smoke goes straight up	Calm	Less than 1
Smoke moves but weather vanes do not	Light Air	1–3
Weather vanes move; leaves rustle	Light Breeze	4–7
Flags flutter; leaves move constantly	Gentle Breeze	8–12
Dirt and paper raised; flags flap	Moderate Breeze	13–18
Small trees sway; flags ripple	Fresh Breeze	19–24
Large branches move; flags beat	Strong Breeze	25–31
Whole trees sway; flags are extended	Moderate Gale	32–38
Twigs break off; hard to walk against	Fresh Gale	39–46
Slight damage to buildings	Strong Gale	47–54
Trees uprooted; windows break	Full Gale	55–63
Widespread damage to buildings	Violent Storm	64–75
General destruction	Hurricane	Over 75

	Observations	Name of wind	Miles per hour
Monday			
Tuesday			
Wednesday			
Thursday			
Friday			

- Which day had the fastest wind? What was the wind speed? _____
- Which day had the slowest wind? What was the wind speed? _____

Adventures in Earth Science, © 1987 David S. Lake Publishers

Name _____

Wind speed is one type of information you can find on a weather map. Use the map and chart below to help you find the wind speed for each city. Then write the name of the city in the column that tells its wind speed.

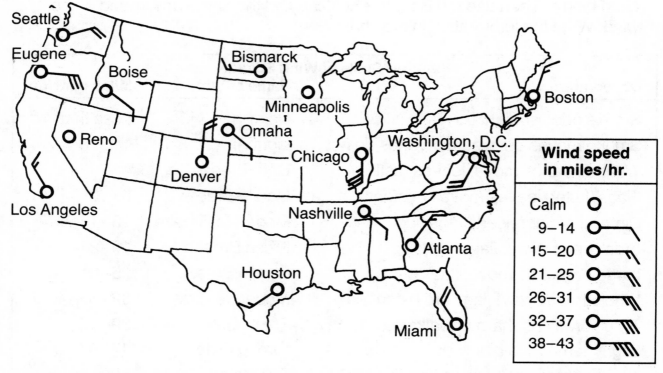

Calm	9–14 mph	15–20 mph	21–25 mph	32–37 mph	38–43 mph

Adventures in Earth Science, © 1987 David S. Lake Publishers

Here Today, Gone Tomorrow

Name _____

The land is constantly changing around you. Many of these changes are caused by erosion and weathering. Look at each set of pictures below. Number them to show the order of the changes.

1. Wind changes the shape of the land.

 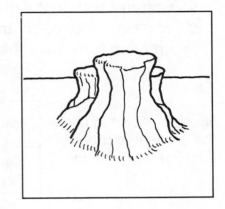 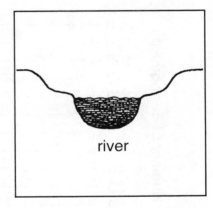

2. Water changes the shape of the land.

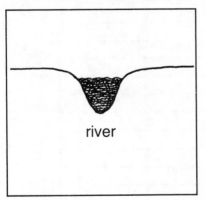 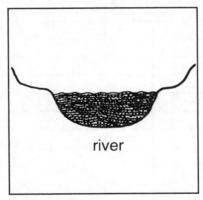 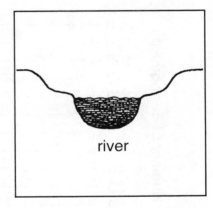

river   river   river

3. Water and ice change the shape of mountains.

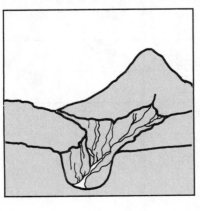 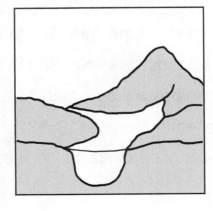 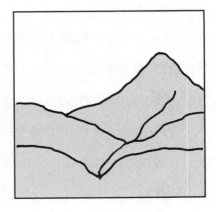

Shake, Rattle, and Roll

Name _____

Many earthquakes have occurred in California. Most of them have done no damage. The information listed below shows the number of earthquakes that occurred in three California areas between the years 1980 and 1985. Plot this information on the graph provided. Use a different color for each area. Then, use the information to answer the questions below.

	1980	1981	1982	1983	1984	1985
Parkfield, CA	104	102	91	89	84	103
San Francisco Peninsula, CA	67	43	66	71	69	59
Mammoth Lakes, CA	185	126	65	61	72	23

Number of earthquakes that measured greater than 3.0 in magnitude

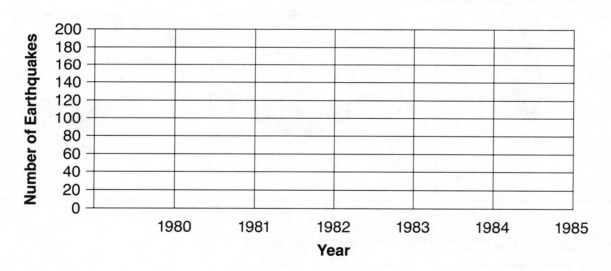

1. Which area had the most earthquakes from 1980 to 1982? _____

2. Which area had the most earthquakes from 1982 to 1985? _____

3. Which area had the fewest earthquakes in 1981? _____

4. Which area had the fewest earthquakes in 1985? _____

5. In which area did the number of earthquakes decrease most from 1980 to 1985? _____

Adventures in Earth Science, © 1987 David S. Lake Publishers

Hot Rocks!

Name _____

Some of the rocks we see come from volcanoes. There are different kinds of volcanic rock. The differences occur because the rocks are formed differently. Read the descriptions of the rocks below. Then decide how and where each rock is formed. Write the name of the rock on the appropriate blank.

Basalt: This type of rock forms when magma pours slowly out of the earth and cools slowly. Basalt has small crystals and sometimes has small holes.

Granite: This type of rock forms under the ground. The magma cools and hardens between layers of rock. Granite has large crystals and a coarse texture.

Obsidian: This type of rock forms when magma pours out of the earth slowly but cools quickly. It looks like smooth, black glass.

Pumice: This type of rock forms when foamy lava cools very quickly. It is full of holes, very light, and can float.

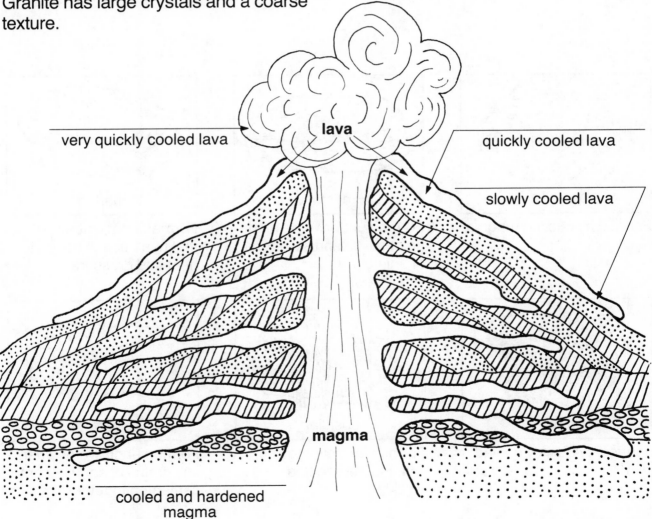

very quickly cooled lava

lava

quickly cooled lava

slowly cooled lava

magma

cooled and hardened magma

Don't Take It for Granite!

Name _____

Scientists often group rocks by the way they were formed. Read the descriptions of the three kinds of rock formation. Then look at the rocks below. Write the name of each rock in the column that describes its formation.

igneous rocks	**sedimentary rocks**	**metamorphic rocks**
Rocks formed by the cooling of hot liquid magma or lava.	Rocks that were formed over a period of time in layers. They are made of the hardened sediments of broken rocks or other materials.	Rocks that began as another kind of rock, but have changed because of pressure and/or heat.

_____

_____

_____

_____

_____

_____

_____

_____

_____

_____

_____

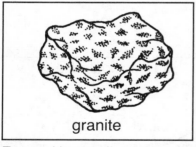

granite

Formed by cooling magma.

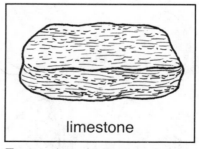

limestone

Formed underwater, made up of shells and skeletons of animals.

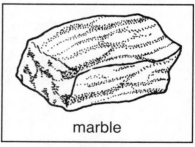

marble

Formed from limestone that has been exposed to heat and pressure.

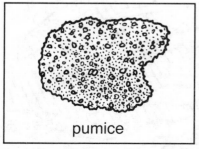

pumice

Formed by quickly cooled lava.

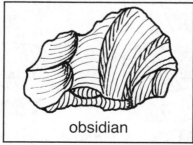

obsidian

Formed by slow-moving lava that has cooled quickly.

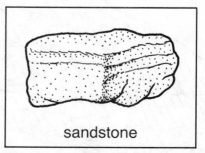

sandstone

Formed underwater when tiny grains of sand become cemented together.

Scratch and Match

Name _____

When you rub certain rocks across a piece of tile, they leave streaks of color. Scientists can sometimes identify the mineral in the rock by the color of the streak. Try this for yourself!

1. Rub a piece of rock across the tile. Record the color it leaves in the chart below. Then look at the color-sorting key and find the mineral the rock contains. Write the mineral name in the chart.
2. Repeat for the remaining rocks.

You will need:

An assortment of rocks

Piece of unglazed tile

Pen or pencil

Rock	Streak Color	Mineral
1		
2		
3		
4		
5		
6		
7		
8		

Color-Sorting Key

Color	Mineral	Color	Mineral
light blue	azurite	yellow-brown	limonite
greenish black	chalcopyrite	black	magnetite
bright red	cinnabar	green	malachite
lead gray	galena	green	olivine
red-brown	hematite	greenish black	pyrite

Telling Time with Fossils

Name _____

Scientists can "see back in time" using fossils. Old fossils tell us something about the earth's past. Some fossils are more than two billion years old. Create a fossil time line. Look at the pictures below. Then write the name of each creature under its age on the time line.

Cephalaspis
≈ 410 million
years old

Eohippus
≈ 50 million
years old

Australopithecus
≈ 2 million years old

Trilobite
≈ 600 million
years old

Dimetrodon
≈ 275 million
years old

Stegasaurus
≈ 150 million
years old

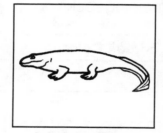

Ichthyostega
≈ 365 million years old

Diatryma
≈ 65 million
years old

Millions of years ago

| 600 | 500 | 400 | 300 | 200 | 100 | 50 | 0 |

410   365   275   150   65   2

Name _____

There are many ways to group animals. This activity will show you one way.
1. Color the labels as marked.
2. Cut out the labels.
3. Listen for directions.

Color these labels red:

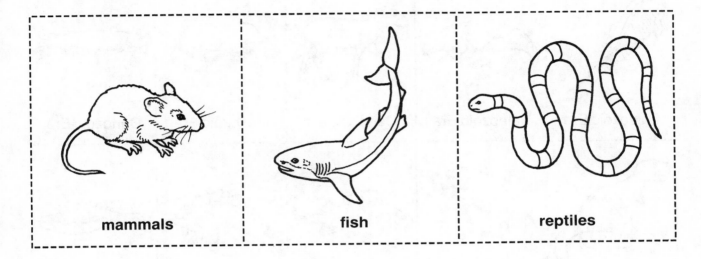

| mammals | fish | reptiles |

Color these labels yellow:

| **Paleozoic Era**
600 million years ago to 230 million years ago | **Mesozoic Era**
230 million years ago to 63 million years ago | **Cenozoic Era**
63 million years ago to present time |

Fossil Circles

You will use these cards with the labels on page 35.
1. Cut out the cards.
2. Listen for directions.

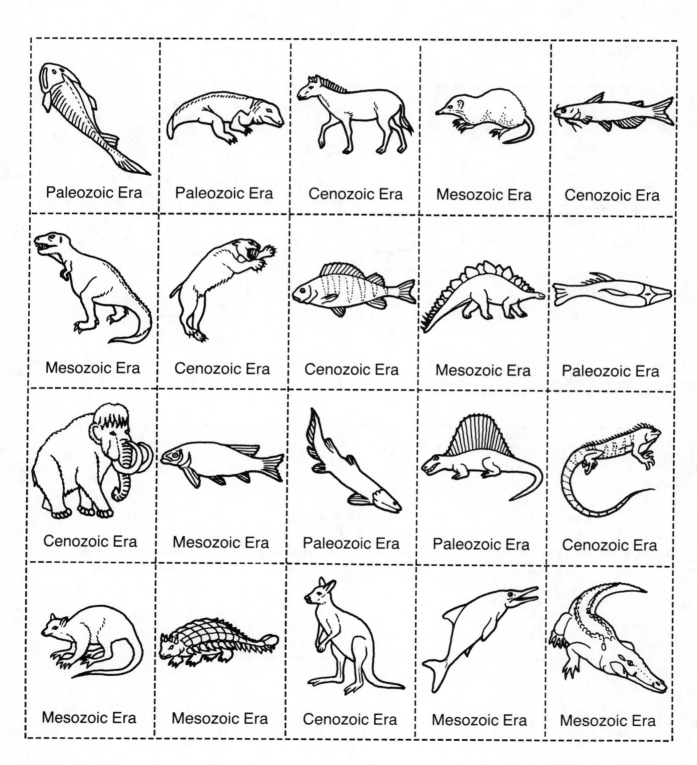

Paleozoic Era	Paleozoic Era	Cenozoic Era	Mesozoic Era	Cenozoic Era
Mesozoic Era	Cenozoic Era	Cenozoic Era	Mesozoic Era	Paleozoic Era
Cenozoic Era	Mesozoic Era	Paleozoic Era	Paleozoic Era	Cenozoic Era
Mesozoic Era	Mesozoic Era	Cenozoic Era	Mesozoic Era	Mesozoic Era

Adventures in Earth Science, © 1987 David S. Lake Publishers

Inside or Out?

Read the information about each planet. Decide whether it is an inner planet (less than 145,000,000 miles from the Sun) or an outer planet (more than 145,000,000 miles from the Sun). Write *inner* or *outer* on the blank below each planet.

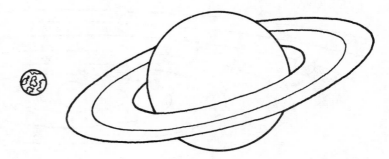

Jupiter
distance from Sun:
484,000,000 miles

Mars
distance from Sun:
142,000,000 miles

Saturn
distance from Sun:
886,000,000 miles

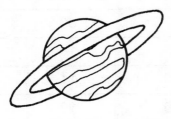

Uranus
distance from Sun:
1,780,000,000 miles

Earth
distance from Sun:
92,956,524 miles

Mercury
distance from Sun:
36,000,000 miles

Pluto
distance from Sun:
3,660,000,000 miles

Neptune
distance from Sun:
2,800,000,000 miles

Venus
distance from Sun:
67,200,000 miles

As the Worlds Turn

Each planet takes a different amount of time to make a complete circle around the Sun. For example, it takes about 365 days for Earth to circle the Sun. But it takes about 88 days for Mercury to circle the Sun, and 90,700 days for Pluto to circle the Sun. Use the following information to help you answer the questions below.

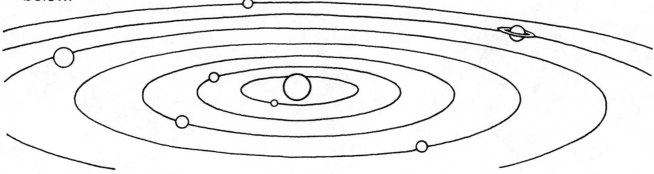

If you were this many
Earth-years old:

You would be this many years old
if you lived on:

Earth	Mercury	Mars	Jupiter	Uranus
8	33	4	.6	.08
9	37	4.5	.7	.09
10	41	5	.8	.1
11	42	5.5	.9	.11
12	49	6	1.0	.12

1. If you were 8 Earth-years old, how many Mercury-years old would you be?

_____

2. If you were 10 Earth-years old, how many Uranus-years old would you be?

_____

3. If you were 12 Earth-years old, how many Mars-years old would you be?

_____

4. If you were 41 Mercury-years old, how many Jupiter-years old would you be?

_____

5. If you were 1 Jupiter-year old, how many Earth-years old would you be?

_____

6. How many Mars-years old are you?

_____

Adventures in Earth Science, © 1987 David S. Lake Publishers

Faces of the Moon

Name _____

The pictures below show the positions of the moon over a period of a month. The names of the phases we see on earth are written next to each circle. In each circle, draw what the moon would look like from earth during that phase. (The first two are done for you.)

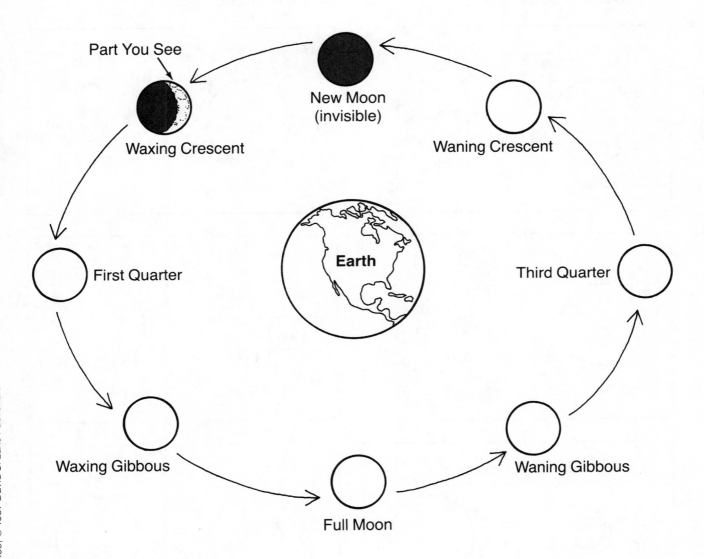

Part You See

New Moon
(invisible)

Waxing Crescent

Waning Crescent

First Quarter

Earth

Third Quarter

Waxing Gibbous

Waning Gibbous

Full Moon

Eclipse It!

When the moon blocks the sun's light and casts a shadow on the earth, we see a *solar eclipse*. When the earth blocks the sun's light and casts a shadow on the moon, we see a *lunar eclipse*.

Circle the picture that shows the positions of the moon, earth, and sun during a solar eclipse.

Circle the picture that shows the positions of the moon, earth, and sun during a lunar eclipse.

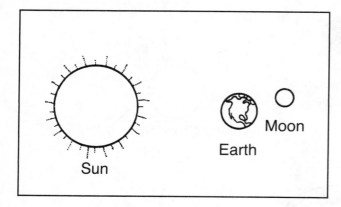

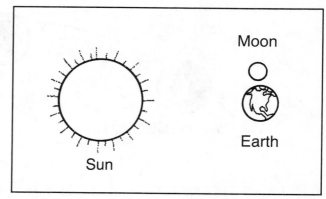

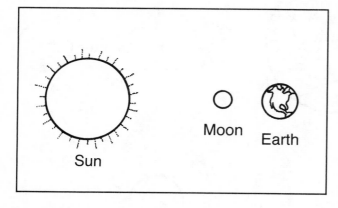

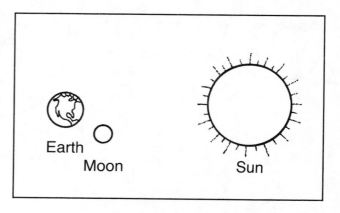

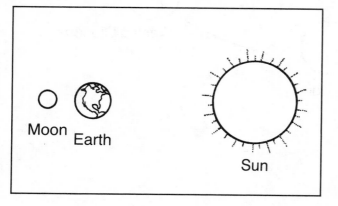

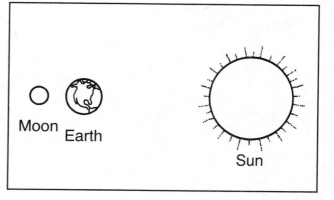

Adventures in Earth Science, © 1987 David S. Lake Publishers

The Constellation Game

Name _____

Look at the stars in each circle. Can you see any pictures in the stars? When you do, draw lines to connect the stars. Give your constellation a name. Write it on the blank below the circle.

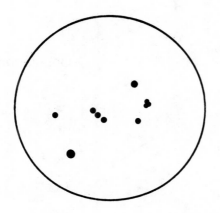

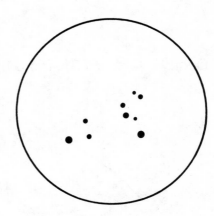

1. _____   2. _____

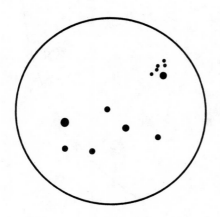

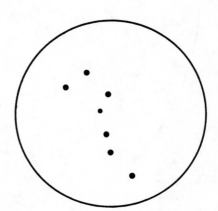

3. _____   4. _____

Starry, Starry Sight

Name _____

The following are constellations we can see in the sky. Look at them closely and then try to find each constellation on the star map below. Draw lines to connect the stars in each constellation you find.

Orion   The Big Dipper   Leo   Cassiopeia

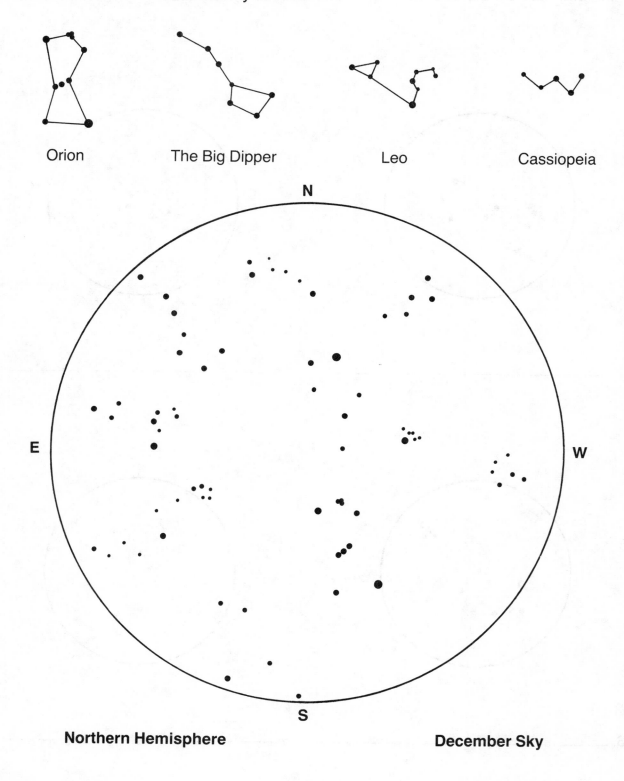

Northern Hemisphere   **December Sky**

How Hot Is Red?

Name _____

Scientists sometimes classify stars by their colors. Each color is associated with a temperature range. Use the following information to fill in the bar graph below.

- Blue stars have a temperature of 34,000°C or more.
- Yellow stars range in temperature from 5,000°C to 6,000°C.
- Blue-white stars range in temperature from 11,000°C to 34,000°C.
- Red stars have a temperature of 4,000°C or less.
- White stars range in temperature from 8,000°C to 11,000°C.
- Orange stars range in temperature from 4,000°C to 5,000°C.
- Yellow-white stars range in temperature from 6,000°C to 8,000°C.

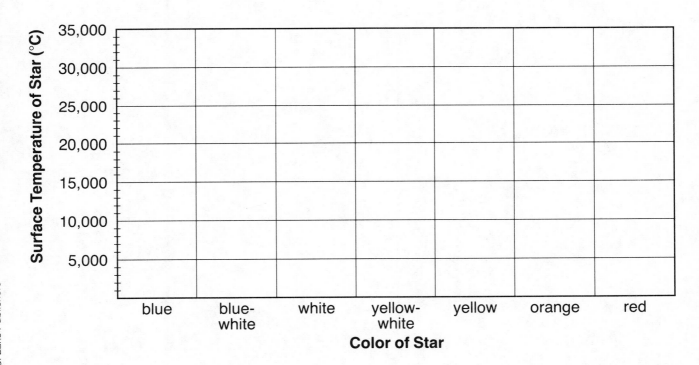

1. Which type of star is the coolest? _____

2. Our sun is a yellow star. How hot is it? _____

3. Sirius is 10,500°C. What color is it? _____

4. Rigel is 12,000°C. What color is it? _____

Doing Science

Adventures in Physical Science

Process-Oriented Activities for Grades 4–6

CONTENTS

TEACHER'S GUIDE

Changing Matter

Concept

Matter can be changed.

Process Emphasis

Observing and collecting data

Materials

For each student:
- Activity worksheet, page 24
- Pencil or pen

For each group of five students:
- Eight paper cups
- Water
- Eight different materials (Suggested materials are: a tea bag, a piece of steel wool, a spoonful of oil, a piece of soap, a seltzer tablet, a dried bean, a piece of tissue paper, a spoonful of salt)
- A spoon

Procedure

1. Explain that matter can change in many ways. Ask students for examples and discuss their suggestions. Point out that matter changes because of the conditions that surround it or because of the substances it contacts.

2. Divide the class into groups of five and hand out the materials. Lead students through the directions on the worksheet. Once they have completed the activity they should answer the questions at the bottom of the page. (You might ask them to suggest

ways in which some of the materials can be changed back into their original forms.)

3. If you want, discuss the differences between a physical change (one that changes the appearance but not the composition of a substance) and a chemical change (one that changes the composition of a substance).

Discovery Questions

- Could the changes that you observed have happened if you hadn't added water?
- How could the changes be speeded up?
- How could the changes be slowed down?

Changing Matter

Name _____

1. Your teacher will give you eight different objects. Put one in each cup. Fill each cup half full of water.
2. Stir the contents of each cup and record what happens to the object.
3. Let your cups sit overnight. Observe the changes that occurred and record them.

You will need:
Eight paper cups
Water
Eight different materials
Pencil

Material	What happened right after adding water	What happened after a day

- Can any of the materials be changed back into their original forms? If so, which ones? _____
- Are any of the changes permanent? If so, which ones? _____

24

Name That Change!

Concept

Matter undergoes two main types of change—physical change and chemical change.

Process Emphasis

Classifying

Materials

For each student:
- Activity worksheet, page 25
- Pen or pencil

For the class:
- Several pieces of paper
- Scissors
- Match
- Tweezers
- Metal pan

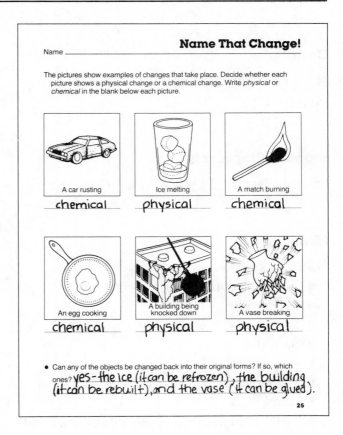

Procedure

1. Crumple a piece of paper into a ball. Ask students if the change you made resulted in a new material or if the material is the same as when you started. Now cut the paper into small pieces and repeat the question. Finally burn a small piece of the paper over the metal pan. Repeat the question. Explain that if you change the appearance of a substance (for instance, crumpling the paper or cutting it) but not the composition of the substance, you have made a change called a physical change. If you change the composition (for instance, burning the paper, which changes it into carbon dioxide and water) you have made a chemical change. Review other examples of the two changes.

2. Hand out the worksheet. Have students classify each change shown as a physical change or a chemical change.

Discovery Questions

- How could you physically change an egg?
- How could you chemically change an egg?

Salt or Sugar?

Concept

Matter has physical properties that can be observed.

Process Emphasis

Comparing and drawing conclusions

Materials

For each student:
- Activity worksheet, page 26
- Pen or pencil
- Labeled samples of sugar and salt
- Spoon
- Water
- Three paper cups
- Hand lens
- Unlabeled sample of *either* sugar or salt

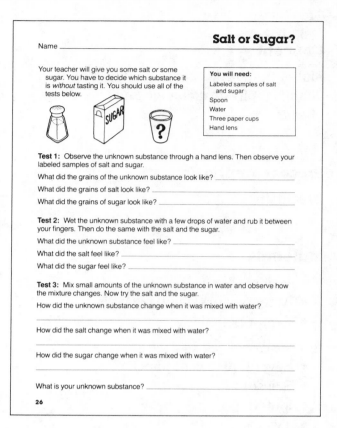

Procedure

1. Ask students to compare sugar and salt. (Most students will probably start by comparing the taste of the two substances.) Then ask them if they can think of any other ways besides taste to tell the difference between the two. Point out that both sugar and salt have properties that can be observed. (You may have to discuss the meaning of the word *property.*) Even though salt and sugar may look alike, if they are magnified they might look different. The feel of the two substances might be different, or the substances might behave differently when heated.

2. Hand out the materials. Remind students that they should never taste unknown substances, even if they think they know what the substances are. Lead students through the directions on the worksheet. When the class is finished, discuss the results.

Discovery Questions

- Why should you use more than one test to determine what a substance is?
- What are some other tests we could try?

The Litmus Test

Concept

Indicators can be used to identify acids, bases, or neutral solutions.

Process Emphasis

Collecting data, comparing, and drawing conclusions

Materials

For each student:
- Activity worksheet, page 27
- Pen or pencil

For each group of four students:
- Ten different samples of acids, bases, and neutrals
  Examples:
  Acids: lemon juice, aspirin-water, vinegar-water, pickle juice
  Bases: bleach-water, ammonia-water, soap-water, baking soda–water, milk of magnesia
  Neutrals: milk, plain water, neutralized mixture of an acid and a base (lemon juice mixed with baking soda)
- Ten paper cups
- Several strips of red and blue litmus paper

Procedure

1. Discuss acids, bases, and neutral solutions. Ask students if they know of any ways to find out if a solution is an acid or a base. Point out that students should never taste a substance to find out if it is an acid or a base. Explain that litmus paper contains a material called an indicator. It indicates, or shows, whether a substance is an acid or a base.

The Litmus Test

Name _____

What dissolves in water and forms an acid solution? A base solution? A neutral solution? Try this experiment and find out!

1. Your teacher will put a different substance in each cup. Write the name of the substance on the cup and under the *substance* column in the chart.
2. Guess whether each substance forms an acid, base, or neutral solution. Write your guess in the chart.
3. Use the litmus paper to test each solution. Record the color that the red and blue papers turn in the chart. Then use the Color Key to help you decide what type of solution each substance forms. Write the result in the chart.

You will need:
Ten substances dissolved in water
Ten paper cups
Red litmus paper
Blue litmus paper

Substance	Guess	Color of red litmus	Color of blue litmus	Type of solution

Color Key		
The solution is **acid** if:	The solution is **base** if:	The solution is **neutral** if:
red litmus remains **red** blue litmus turns **red**	red litmus turns **blue** blue litmus remains **blue**	red litmus remains **red** blue litmus remains **blue**

27

2. Hand out the materials. Tell students which substance is in each cup. Have them label the cups and write the names of the substances on their charts. Tell students that before they check each substance, they should guess (predict) whether the substance is an acid, a base, or a neutral solution. Have them record their guesses. When they have finished, they should test each solution using the litmus paper and record the answers.

Discovery Questions

- What are some ways in which acids are used?
- What are some ways in which bases are used?
- Why should you never taste a substance to determine whether it is an acid or a base?

Forceful Fields

Concept

Magnets have magnetic fields that surround them.

Process Emphasis

Collecting data and comparing

Materials

For each student:
- Activity worksheet, page 28
- Pen or pencil

For each pair of students:
- Two bar magnets
- Sheet of paper
- Iron filings (or finely snipped steel wool)
- Newspaper

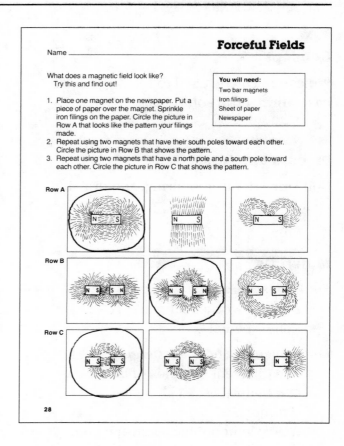

Procedure

1. Divide the class into pairs. Hand out the materials and lead students through the directions on the worksheet. (Students may have to try several times to get a clean picture of the magnets' fields.)

2. When students have completed the activity, discuss magnetic fields. Explain that the bar magnet attracts some iron filings and makes others line up around it. The region around the magnet that acts on the iron filings is the magnetic field.

Discovery Questions

- Do you think that a magnetic field around a horseshoe magnet would look the same as a field around a bar magnet?
- Do you think that the magnetic field of a stronger magnet would look the same as the magnetic field of a weaker magnet of the same shape?

A Magnetic Attraction

Concept

Magnets have different strengths.

Process Emphasis

Measuring and collecting data

Materials

For each student:
- Activity worksheet, page 29
- Pen or pencil

For each group of three students:
- Three different magnets labeled 1, 2, and 3
- Thirty small paper clips
- One large paper clip

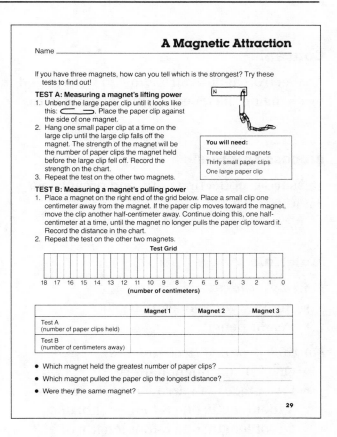

A Magnetic Attraction

Name _____

If you have three magnets, how can you tell which is the strongest? Try these tests to find out!

TEST A: Measuring a magnet's lifting power
1. Unbend the large paper clip until it looks like this: ⊂═══⊃. Place the paper clip against the side of one magnet.
2. Hang one small paper clip at a time on the large clip until the large clip falls off the magnet. The strength of the magnet will be the number of paper clips the magnet held before the large clip fell off. Record the strength on the chart.
3. Repeat the test on the other two magnets.

You will need:
Three labeled magnets
Thirty small paper clips
One large paper clip

TEST B: Measuring a magnet's pulling power
1. Place a magnet on the right end of the grid below. Place a small clip one centimeter away from the magnet. If the paper clip moves toward the magnet, move the clip another half-centimeter away. Continue doing this, one half-centimeter at a time, until the magnet no longer pulls the paper clip toward it. Record the distance in the chart.
2. Repeat the test on the other two magnets.

Test Grid

18 17 16 15 14 13 12 11 10 9 8 7 6 5 4 3 2 1 0
(number of centimeters)

	Magnet 1	Magnet 2	Magnet 3
Test A (number of paper clips held)			
Test B (number of centimeters away)			

- Which magnet held the greatest number of paper clips? _____
- Which magnet pulled the paper clip the longest distance? _____
- Were they the same magnet? _____

29

Procedure

1. Divide the class into groups of three. Hand each group the three magnets. Have them examine the magnets, and then ask them if they can tell you which magnet is the strongest. Discuss their answers.

2. Hand out the rest of the materials and the worksheet. Explain that they can measure the strength of each magnet using the materials. Guide students through the worksheet directions.

Discovery Questions

- What would happen to the strength of the magnets if we used heavier paper clips?
- What are some other units of measure we could use instead of paper clips?

How Strong Is It?

Concept

An electromagnet's strength can be changed by changing the length of the winding wire.

Process Emphasis

Measuring, collecting data, and organizing data

Materials

For each student:

- Activity worksheet, page 30
- Pen or pencil

For each group of two students:

- One "D" flashlight battery
- Five pieces of narrow gauge wire—one 2-foot length; one 3-foot length; one 4-foot length; one 5-foot length; one 6-foot length
- Forty small paper clips
- One large paper clip
- One iron nail or screw (1½-2½ inches long)
- Wire stripper

Procedure

1. Demonstrate how to build an electromagnet. Strip about 1 inch of insulation from each end of the wire pieces. Use the 2-foot piece of wire. Leave about 3 inches of wire free on both ends. Carefully wind the wire as tightly as possible around the screw or nail (see Figure A). When each end of the wire is placed against the end of the battery, the nail becomes a magnet. (Remind students not to keep the magnet on too long or the battery will wear out.)

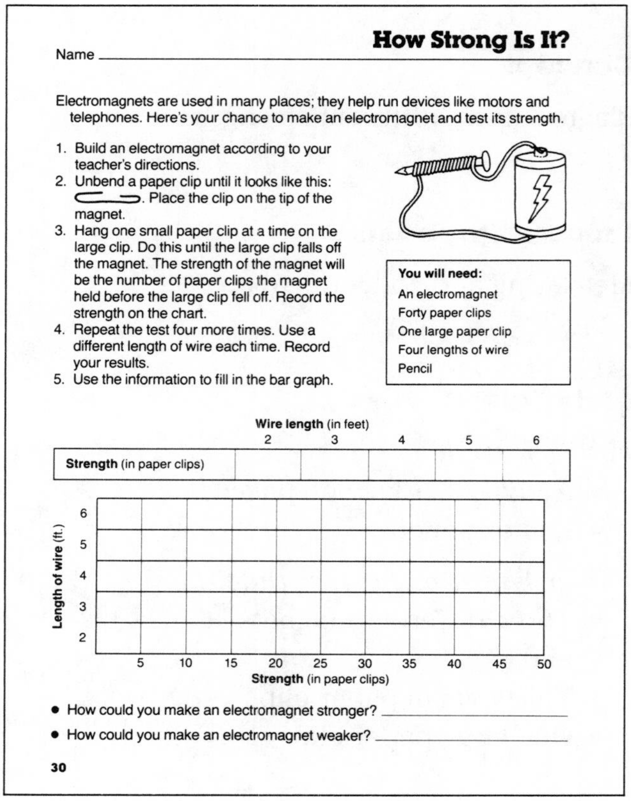

How Strong Is It?

Name ______________________________

Electromagnets are used in many places; they help run devices like motors and telephones. Here's your chance to make an electromagnet and test its strength.

1. Build an electromagnet according to your teacher's directions.
2. Unbend a paper clip until it looks like this: ⊂⊃. Place the clip on the tip of the magnet.
3. Hang one small paper clip at a time on the large clip. Do this until the large clip falls off the magnet. The strength of the magnet will be the number of paper clips the magnet held before the large clip fell off. Record the strength on the chart.
4. Repeat the test four more times. Use a different length of wire each time. Record your results.
5. Use the information to fill in the bar graph.

You will need:
An electromagnet
Forty paper clips
One large paper clip
Four lengths of wire
Pencil

Wire length (in feet)	2	3	4	5	6
Strength (in paper clips)					

Length of wire (ft.): 6, 5, 4, 3, 2
Strength (in paper clips): 5, 10, 15, 20, 25, 30, 35, 40, 45, 50

- How could you make an electromagnet stronger? ______________
- How could you make an electromagnet weaker? ______________

30

2. Divide the class into groups of two and hand out the materials. Have each group make an electromagnet. Then guide students through the worksheet directions.

Discovery Questions

- Can you think of any other ways to make an electromagnet stronger? If so, what are they?
- How are magnets and electromagnets similar?
- How are magnets and electromagnets different?

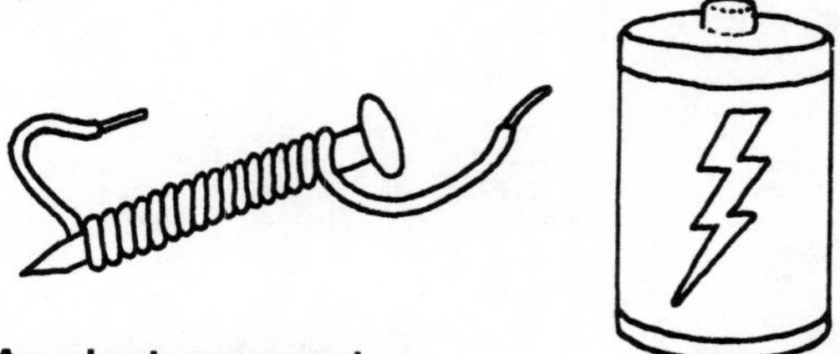

Figure A: An electromagnet

What Type of Circuit?

Concept

There are two types of electrical circuits—*series* circuits and *parallel* circuits.

Process Emphasis

Classifying

Materials

For each student:
- Activity worksheet, page 31
- Pen or pencil

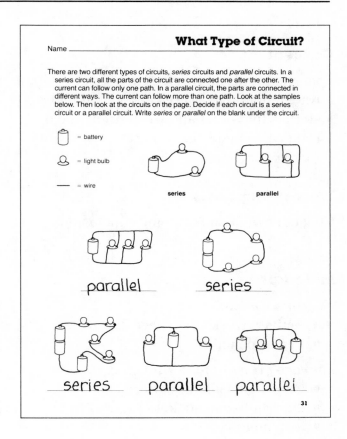

What Type of Circuit?

Name _____

There are two different types of circuits, *series* circuits and *parallel* circuits. In a series circuit, all the parts of the circuit are connected one after the other. The current can follow only one path. In a parallel circuit, the parts are connected in different ways. The current can follow more than one path. Look at the samples below. Then look at the circuits on the page. Decide if each circuit is a series circuit or a parallel circuit. Write *series* or *parallel* on the blank under the circuit.

= battery

= light bulb

= wire

series   parallel

parallel   series

series   parallel   parallel

31

Procedure

1. Discuss the parts of an electrical circuit. Point out that a circuit usually has at least three parts—a source of electrical energy (batteries), a path of material for the current to travel in (wire), and something that uses the current (light bulb). Explain that there are two types of circuits—series circuits and parallel circuits. You might want to discuss the similarities and differences between the two circuits.

2. Hand out the worksheet. Have students classify each circuit as a series circuit or a parallel circuit.

Discovery Questions

- What happens if one part of the circuit is missing?
- Suppose you had a series circuit with one battery and two light bulbs. What would happen if one of the light bulbs burnt out?
- Suppose you had a parallel circuit with one battery and two light bulbs. What would happen if one of the light bulbs burnt out?

Conductors and Insulators

Concept

Some materials allow electricity to go through them. These are called *conductors*. Materials that don't allow electricity to go through are called *insulators*.

Process Emphasis

Collecting data and drawing conclusions

Materials

For each student:
- Activity worksheet, page 32
- Pen or pencil

For each group of four students:
- One "D" flashlight battery
- Light bulb and socket
- Insulated wire
- Electrical tape
- Aluminum foil
- Door key
- Paper cup
- Nickel
- Rubber band
- Pencil
- Wood or plastic ruler

Procedure

1. Set up the circuit shown on the worksheet (page 32). Touch the two ends of the wire together. Explain that the electricity moves from one end of the battery to the other along the wire. The wire is called a conductor. It conducts electricity. Ask

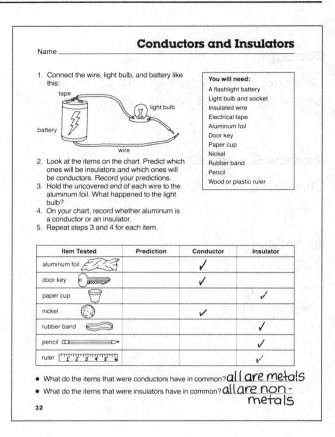

students if they can think of any other conductors. You should also discuss insulators.

2. Divide the class into groups of four and hand out the materials. Explain to students that they will be making a conductor tester. Guide students through the worksheet directions.

Discovery Questions

- What are some of the things we use insulators for?
- What are some of the things we use conductors for?

Seeing Your Voice

Concept

The pitch of a sound and the rate of vibration of the sound are directly related.

Process Emphasis

Observing, collecting data, and drawing conclusions

Materials

For each student:
- Activity worksheet, page 33
- Pen or pencil

For each group of two students:
- Coffee can or oatmeal container
- Can opener (if using coffee can)
- Scissors
- Large balloon
- Small piece of mirror (1–2 cm square)
- White glue
- Rubber band
- Flashlight (if it's a rainy day)

Procedure

1. Ask students if they can think of any ways to make sounds visible. Explain that one way to "see" the sound waves of your voice is to make a soundscope.

2. Divide the class into groups of two and hand out the materials. Have each group make a soundscope as described on page 33. Guide the students through the rest of the directions on the page.

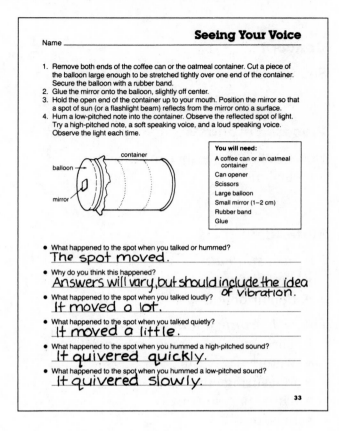

Name _____

Seeing Your Voice

1. Remove both ends of the coffee can or the oatmeal container. Cut a piece of the balloon large enough to be stretched tightly over one end of the container. Secure the balloon with a rubber band.
2. Glue the mirror onto the balloon, slightly off center.
3. Hold the open end of the container up to your mouth. Position the mirror so that a spot of sun (or a flashlight beam) reflects from the mirror onto a surface.
4. Hum a low-pitched note into the container. Observe the reflected spot of light. Try a high-pitched note, a soft speaking voice, and a loud speaking voice. Observe the light each time.

You will need:
A coffee can or an oatmeal container
Can opener
Scissors
Large balloon
Small mirror (1–2 cm)
Rubber band
Glue

- What happened to the spot when you talked or hummed?
  The spot moved.
- Why do you think this happened?
  Answers will vary, but should include the idea of vibration.
- What happened to the spot when you talked loudly?
  It moved a lot.
- What happened to the spot when you talked quietly?
  It moved a little.
- What happened to the spot when you hummed a high-pitched sound?
  It quivered quickly.
- What happened to the spot when you hummed a low-pitched sound?
  It quivered slowly.

33

3. When the students have finished experimenting with their soundscopes, ask them if they can explain how the soundscope works. (The disturbance caused by the voice causes a stream of air to vibrate. The vibrating air hits the balloon and causes the balloon and the mirror to vibrate. The distance the light beam moves shows the loudness of the noise. The rate at which it quivers shows the pitch of the noise.)

Discovery Questions

- How is the balloon on the soundscope like an eardrum?

Playing with Pitch

Concept

Sounds differ in pitch.

Process Emphasis

Observing, comparing, and drawing conclusions

Materials

For each student:
- Activity worksheet, page 34
- Pen or pencil

For each group of four students:
- Three glasses (same size and shape)
- Water
- Measuring cup
- Three paper straws
- Scissors
- Three thicknesses of rubber bands
- Shoe box (without top)
- Spoon

Procedure

1. Divide the class into groups of four. Hand out the materials and lead students through the directions on the worksheet.

2. When students have finished the worksheet, discuss their results. Explain that the lowness or the highness of a sound is its *pitch*. The pitch of a sound is determined by how rapidly the source of the

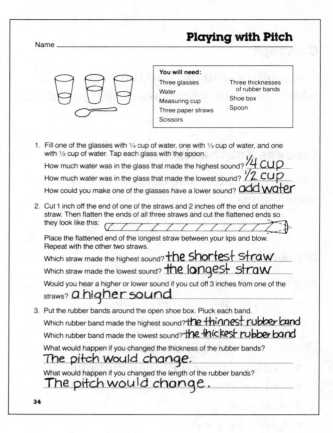

sound is vibrating. Point out that something that vibrates slowly produces a lower note and something that vibrates rapidly produces a higher note. You might want to tell students that the speed at which something vibrates is called its *frequency*.

Discovery Questions

- What are the lowest and highest frequencies that people can hear?
- Why can cats and dogs hear sounds that we can't hear?

Sequencing Sounds

Concept

Sounds can be arranged according to pitch.

Process Emphasis

Sequencing

Materials

For each student:
- Activity worksheet, page 35
- Pen or pencil

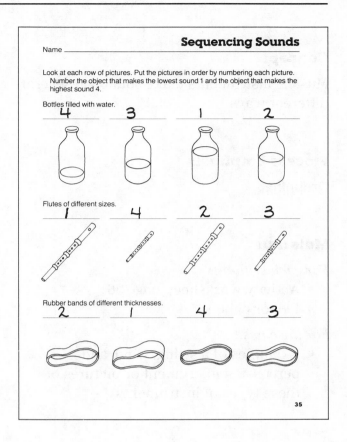

Sequencing Sounds

Name _____

Look at each row of pictures. Put the pictures in order by numbering each picture. Number the object that makes the lowest sound 1 and the object that makes the highest sound 4.

Bottles filled with water.

4   3   1   2

Flutes of different sizes.

1   4   2   3

Rubber bands of different thicknesses.

2   1   4   3

35

Procedure

1. Review the concept of pitch. Explain that something that vibrates slowly produces a lower note and something that vibrates quickly produces a higher note. You might want to discuss musical scales and how the scales are arranged by pitch.

2. Hand out the worksheet. Have students sequence the pictures by the pitch of the sounds the objects make. The lowest sound should be numbered 1 and the highest sound should be numbered 4.

Discovery Questions

- What are some things that make sounds with high pitches?
- What are some things that make sounds with low pitches?

Making Music

Concept

Musical instruments make sounds in several different ways.

Process Emphasis

Grouping

Materials

For each student:
- Activity worksheet, page 36
- Pen or pencil

For the class:
- Examples of a string, wind, and percussion instrument or pictures of these types of instruments

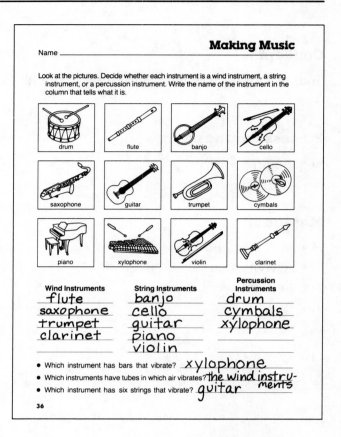

Procedure

1. Show students the three instruments or the pictures of the instruments. Ask them if they can tell you how the instruments make sounds. Discuss their answers and explain that the string instrument makes sounds because its strings vibrate, the wind instrument makes sounds because the column of air inside the tube vibrates, and the percussion instrument makes sounds because the object which is struck vibrates.

2. Hand out the worksheet. Have students write the name of each instrument in the appropriate category.

Discovery Questions

- What happens in all musical instruments that produce sound?
- How are voices like musical instruments?

14

Turning Up the Volume

Concept

The loudness of a sound can be measured in decibels.

Process Emphasis

Organizing data

Materials

For each student:
- Activity worksheet, page 37
- Pen or pencil

For the class:
- Piece of string

Procedure

1. Explain that when something vibrates and creates a sound, it moves back and forth past its original resting place. Demonstrate how this looks using the piece of string. Point out to students that the distance the string moves from its resting place is its *amplitude* (see Figure A). Loud sounds have big amplitudes and soft sounds have small amplitudes. Discuss the fact that scientists can measure the amplitude, or loudness, of a sound using a sound-level meter. The unit used to measure the loudness of sound is called the *decibel*.

2. Hand out the worksheet. Have students fill in the graph using the information on the page. When they have finished the graph they should answer the questions at the bottom of the page.

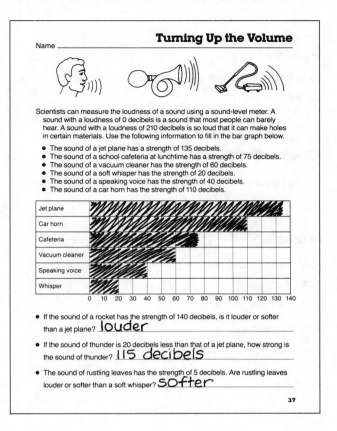

Discovery Questions

- What happens to your body when you hear loud sounds (over 70 decibels)?
- What is noise pollution?

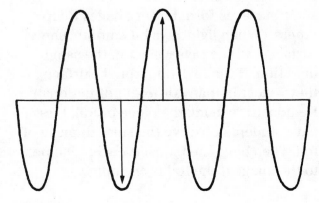

Figure A   **Amplitude**

Upon Reflection . . .

Concept

Light will reflect off a smooth surface to produce an image.

Process Emphasis

Classifying

Materials

For each student:
- Activity worksheet, page 38
- Pen or pencil

For the class:
- Aluminum foil

Upon Reflection . . .

Name _____

Look at each object on the page. Decide if the object reflects an image. If it does, write *image* under the object. If it doesn't, write *no image* under the object.

no image   image   image

no image   no image   no image

image   image   image

38

Procedure

1. Ask students to look around the room and identify objects that will reflect images. Explain that the images form when light bounces off a smooth surface. Discuss why some surfaces form better images than others. (When light rays hit smooth, shiny surfaces, all the rays reflect in the same direction. If the rays hit a rough surface, they reflect in many different directions.) Demonstrate using the piece of foil. First have students observe the smooth piece of foil. Then have them observe what happens to the image if the foil is crumpled.

2. Hand out the worksheet. Have students decide whether each object on the page reflects an image. They should write *image* or *no image* under each item.

Discovery Questions

- What kind of reflections do you see in a curved reflective surface (such as a teakettle or a hubcap)?
- Why is writing backward in a mirror?

Looking Through Lenses

Concept

Light bends when it goes through lenses.

Process Emphasis

Observing and drawing conclusions

Materials

For each student:

- Activity worksheet, page 39
- Three lenses—one flat, one concave, and one convex
- Five objects to look at (pencil, eraser, lettering on notebook, and so on)
- Pen or pencil

Procedure

1. Explain that a lens is a smooth piece of glass or plastic. When light goes through a lens, the light bends in special ways. Some lenses bend light so things look bigger. Some lenses bend light so things look smaller.

2. Hand out the materials. Have students follow the directions on the worksheet. When they have finished testing the lenses, they should answer the questions on the bottom of the page.

3. When the class is finished, you might want to explain how the lenses refract light.

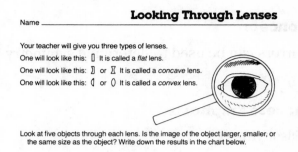

Looking Through Lenses

Name _____

Your teacher will give you three types of lenses.
One will look like this: ⎕ It is called a *flat* lens.
One will look like this: ⎬ or ⎱ It is called a *concave* lens.
One will look like this: ⎨ or ⎰ It is called a *convex* lens.

Look at five objects through each lens. Is the image of the object larger, smaller, or the same size as the object? Write down the results in the chart below.

	Flat Lens Larger, smaller, or same size?	Concave Lens Larger, smaller, or same size?	Convex Lens Larger, smaller, or same size?
Object 1	same size	smaller	larger
Object 2	same size	smaller	larger
Object 3	same size	smaller	larger
Object 4	same size	smaller	larger
Object 5	same size	smaller	larger

- What happens to the image of an object when you look at it through a flat lens? It stays the same size.
- What happens to the image of an object when you look at it through a concave lens? It becomes smaller.
- What happens to the image of an object when you look at it through a convex lens? It becomes larger.

39

Discovery Questions

- What type of lens do you think is in a microscope?
- What type of lens do you think is in a magnifying glass?
- What type of lens do you think is in a telescope?

Is It Symmetrical?

Concept

Mirrors can be used to determine symmetry.

Process Emphasis

Classifying

Materials

For each student:
- Activity worksheet, page 40
- Pen or pencil
- Pocket mirror

Is It Symmetrical?

Name _____

One way to describe something symmetrical is to say that one side is a mirror image of the other side. Use your mirror to test the objects below. Put the mirror perpendicular to the page and try to find an axis of symmetry. If the design that is created in the reflection looks the same as the real design on the page, the object is symmetrical. Don't forget to test for symmetry along different parts of the object. Write the word *symmetrical* or *asymmetrical* (not symmetrical) below each picture.

symmetrical   asymmetrical   symmetrical

asymmetrical   symmetrical   symmetrical

A   C   8   5
symmetrical asymmetrical symmetrical asymmetrical

40

Procedure

1. Ask students to name things that mirrors can be used for (periscopes, looking at images, microscopes, and so on). Explain that mirrors can also be used to determine whether something is symmetrical or asymmetrical. Discuss symmetry. Point out that the word *symmetry* is used to describe something that has parts on opposite sides that look the same. You may want to draw some examples on the board.

2. Hand out the worksheet and mirrors. Have students experiment with each picture to see if they can find an axis of symmetry. (Some objects have more than one axis of symmetry.) If they can, they should write *symmetrical* on the blank under the picture. If the picture is not symmetrical, students should write *asymmetrical* on the blank.

Discovery Questions

- Are people symmetrical?
- What are some things you can find outside that are symmetrical?

Red + Blue + Green = ?

Concept

All the colors we see are made from a combination of three primary colors—red, blue, and green.*

Process Emphasis

Observing and collecting data

Materials

For each student:

- Activity worksheets, pages 41 and 42
- Red, blue, and green markers or crayons
- Scissors
- 8½″ × 11″ piece of cardboard
- Glue
- Four two-foot-long pieces of string
- Sharp pencil or nail

For the class:

- Prism

Procedure

1. Use the prism to introduce the visible spectrum. Explain that while we can distinguish between many different colors, our eyes are really only able to see three colors—red, blue, and green. From these three colors, our brains are able to "see" all the colors.

2. Hand out the materials. Lead the students through the directions on the worksheet. (Note: some of the colors produced by the spinners may look muddy—this is because the pigments in the markers are not very pure.)

3. When the students have finished the worksheet, ask them if they can explain how

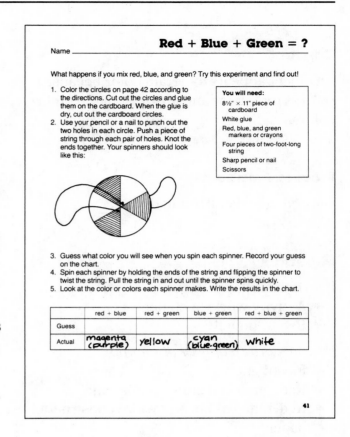

Name _____

Red + Blue + Green = ?

What happens if you mix red, blue, and green? Try this experiment and find out!

1. Color the circles on page 42 according to the directions. Cut out the circles and glue them on the cardboard. When the glue is dry, cut out the cardboard circles.
2. Use your pencil or a nail to punch out the two holes in each circle. Push a piece of string through each pair of holes. Knot the ends together. Your spinners should look like this:

You will need:
8½″ × 11″ piece of cardboard
White glue
Red, blue, and green markers or crayons
Four pieces of two-foot-long string
Sharp pencil or nail
Scissors

3. Guess what color you will see when you spin each spinner. Record your guess on the chart.
4. Spin each spinner by holding the ends of the string and flipping the spinner to twist the string. Pull the string in and out until the spinner spins quickly.
5. Look at the color or colors each spinner makes. Write the results in the chart.

	red + blue	red + green	blue + green	red + blue + green
Guess				
Actual	magenta (purple)	yellow	cyan (blue-green)	white

41

the color spinner works. (The spinner causes your eye to receive different color signals from the same place. They go by so quickly that your eye doesn't see them as flashes of different colors. Instead, it sees two or three signals from the same spot. Your brain combines these into one signal.)

Discovery Questions

- What happens when none of your color receptors receive signals?
- If you stare for a long time at a red spot and then look away, you'll see a green spot. What causes this?

*The primary colors of *light* are red, blue, and green—together these three colors create white light. The primary colors of *pigments* are red, blue, and yellow.

19

Disappearing Colors?

Concept

An object appears a certain color because it reflects that color and absorbs all the other colors.

Process Emphasis

Observing and collecting data

Materials

For each student:
- Activity worksheet, page 43
- Pen or pencil

For each group of four students:
- Flashlight
- Red, blue, and green cellophane
- Red, blue, green, and white construction paper
- Scissors
- Rubber band

Procedure

1. Ask students to make a list of all the colors they can see in the classroom. Darken the room. Ask students to make another list of all the colors that are now visible. Finally ask students what colors would be visible if the room were totally dark. Explain that we see the colors of objects because light is reflected from the object to our eyes. However, not all the light that reaches the objects is reflected. Discuss the primary colors of light (red, blue, and green) and how these colors can be mixed to form other colors.

2. Divide the class into groups of four and hand out the materials. Lead students

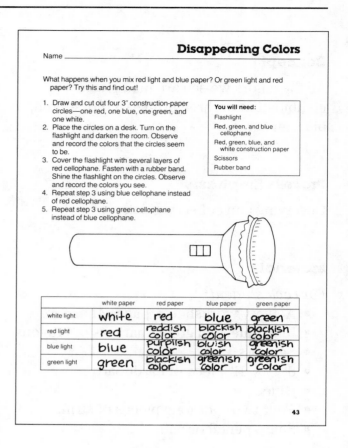

Name _____

Disappearing Colors

What happens when you mix red light and blue paper? Or green light and red paper? Try this and find out!

1. Draw and cut out four 3″ construction-paper circles—one red, one blue, one green, and one white.
2. Place the circles on a desk. Turn on the flashlight and darken the room. Observe and record the colors that the circles seem to be.
3. Cover the flashlight with several layers of red cellophane. Fasten with a rubber band. Shine the flashlight on the circles. Observe and record the colors you see.
4. Repeat step 3 using blue cellophane instead of red cellophane.
5. Repeat step 3 using green cellophane instead of blue cellophane.

You will need:
Flashlight
Red, green, and blue cellophane
Red, green, blue, and white construction paper
Scissors
Rubber band

	white paper	red paper	blue paper	green paper
white light	white	red	blue	green
red light	red	reddish color	blackish color	blackish color
blue light	blue	purplish color	bluish color	greenish color
green light	green	blackish color	greenish color	greenish color

43

through the directions on the worksheet. (You should make the room as dark as possible. Also separate the groups of students so the light from one group doesn't interfere with the light from other groups.)

Discovery Questions

- What color would you see if you mixed red, blue, and green light?
- What color would you see if you mixed red and green light?
- What color would you see if you mixed blue and green light?
- What color would you see if you mixed red and blue light?

Is Seeing Believing?

Concept

Optical illusions occur when the brain misinterprets information from the eyes.

Process Emphasis

Observing and drawing conclusions

Materials

For each student:

- Activity worksheet, page 44
- Pen or pencil

Procedure

1. Hand out the worksheet. Have students answer all the questions on the page.

2. When the students are finished, tell them the answers. Explain that all the pictures on the page are called *optical illusions.* Ask students if they can guess why optical illusions fool us. Discuss their answers. Then explain that optical illusions fool our eyes and our brains. Sometimes our eyes are misled by slanted lines or arrows, so straight lines next to them look longer or shorter than they actually are (Illusions A and B on the worksheet). Sometimes we compare an object to the object right next to it, so a dot inside a large circle looks small while the same dot inside a small circle looks large (Illusion C). Some optical illusions occur

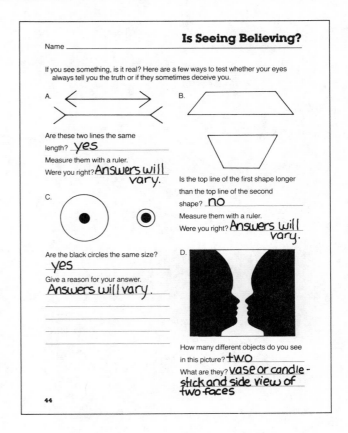

because our brains get confused. We see more than one picture, but our brains aren't sure which picture they want to see (Illusion D).

Discovery Questions

- What is the difference between an illusion and a mirage?
- Why does the moon look larger when it is just above the horizon than it does when it is higher in the sky?

ACTIVITY WORKSHEETS

Changing Matter

1. Your teacher will give you eight different objects. Put one in each cup. Fill each cup half full of water.
2. Stir the contents of each cup and record what happens to the object.
3. Let your cups sit overnight. Observe the changes that occurred and record them.

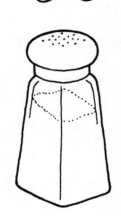

You will need:

Eight paper cups

Water

Eight different materials

Pencil

Material	What happened right after adding water	What happened after a day

- Can any of the materials be changed back into their original forms? If so, which ones? _____
- Are any of the changes permanent? If so, which ones? _____

_____

Adventures in Physical Science, © 1987 David S. Lake Publishers

Name _____

The pictures show examples of changes that take place. Decide whether each picture shows a physical change or a chemical change. Write *physical* or *chemical* in the blank below each picture.

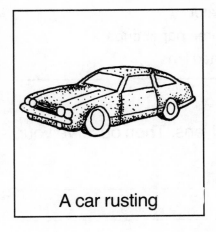

A car rusting

_____

Ice melting

_____

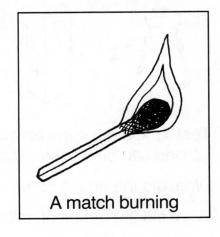

A match burning

_____

An egg cooking

_____

A building being knocked down

_____

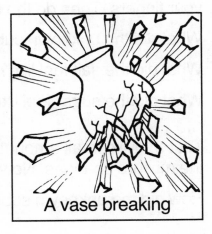

A vase breaking

_____

● Can any of the objects be changed back into their original forms? If so, which

ones? _____

_____

25

Salt or Sugar?

Name _____

Your teacher will give you some salt *or* some sugar. You have to decide which substance it is *without* tasting it. You should use all of the tests below.

Test 1: Observe the unknown substance through a hand lens. Then observe your labeled samples of salt and sugar.

What did the grains of the unknown substance look like? _____

What did the grains of salt look like? _____

What did the grains of sugar look like? _____

Test 2: Wet the unknown substance with a few drops of water and rub it between your fingers. Then do the same with the salt and the sugar.

What did the unknown substance feel like? _____

What did the salt feel like? _____

What did the sugar feel like? _____

Test 3: Mix small amounts of the unknown substance in water and observe how the mixture changes. Now try the salt and the sugar.

How did the unknown substance change when it was mixed with water?

_____

How did the salt change when it was mixed with water?

_____

How did the sugar change when it was mixed with water?

_____

What is your unknown substance? _____

Adventures in Physical Science, © 1987 David S. Lake Publishers

The Litmus Test

Name _____

What dissolves in water and forms an acid solution? A base solution? A neutral solution? Try this experiment and find out!

1. Your teacher will put a different substance in each cup. Write the name of the substance on the cup and under the *substance* column in the chart.
2. Guess whether each substance forms an acid, base, or neutral solution. Write your guess in the chart.
3. Use the litmus paper to test each solution. Record the color that the red and blue papers turn in the chart. Then use the Color Key to help you decide what type of solution each substance forms. Write the result in the chart.

You will need:

Ten substances dissolved in water

Ten paper cups

Red litmus paper

Blue litmus paper

Substance	Guess	Color of red litmus	Color of blue litmus	Type of solution

Color Key		
The solution is **acid** if:	The solution is **base** if:	The solution is **neutral** if:
red litmus remains **red** **blue** litmus turns **red**	**red** litmus turns **blue** **blue** litmus remains **blue**	**red** litmus remains **red** **blue** litmus remains **blue**

Adventures in Physical Science, © 1987 David S. Lake Publishers

Name _____

What does a magnetic field look like?
  Try this and find out!

1. Place one magnet on the newspaper. Put a
    piece of paper over the magnet. Sprinkle
    iron filings on the paper. Circle the picture in
    Row A that looks like the pattern your filings
    made.
2. Repeat using two magnets that have their south poles toward each other.
    Circle the picture in Row B that shows the pattern.
3. Repeat using two magnets that have a north pole and a south pole toward
    each other. Circle the picture in Row C that shows the pattern.

Row A

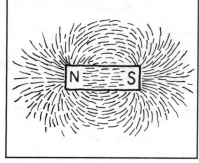 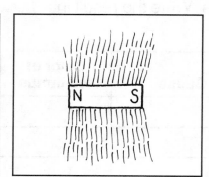 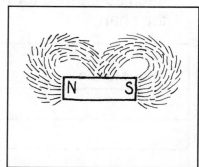

Row B

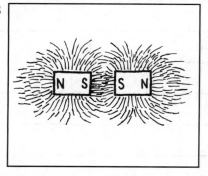 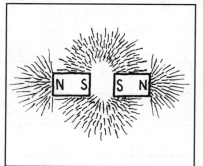 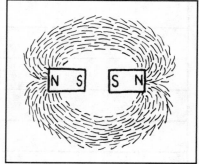

Row C

  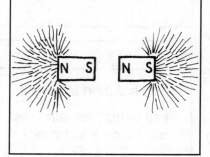

Adventures in Physical Science, © 1987 David S. Lake Publishers

A Magnetic Attraction

Name _____

If you have three magnets, how can you tell which is the strongest? Try these tests to find out!

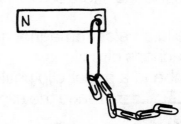

TEST A: Measuring a magnet's lifting power
1. Unbend the large paper clip until it looks like this: ⊂━━⊃. Place the paper clip against the side of one magnet.
2. Hang one small paper clip at a time on the large clip until the large clip falls off the magnet. The strength of the magnet will be the number of paper clips the magnet held before the large clip fell off. Record the strength on the chart.
3. Repeat the test on the other two magnets.

You will need:

Three labeled magnets

Thirty small paper clips

One large paper clip

TEST B: Measuring a magnet's pulling power
1. Place a magnet on the right end of the grid below. Place a small clip one centimeter away from the magnet. If the paper clip moves toward the magnet, move the clip another half-centimeter away. Continue doing this, one half-centimeter at a time, until the magnet no longer pulls the paper clip toward it. Record the distance in the chart.
2. Repeat the test on the other two magnets.

Test Grid

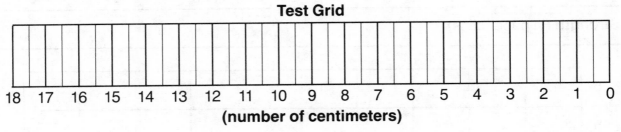

18 17 16 15 14 13 12 11 10 9 8 7 6 5 4 3 2 1 0

(number of centimeters)

	Magnet 1	Magnet 2	Magnet 3
Test A (number of paper clips held)			
Test B (number of centimeters away)			

- Which magnet held the greatest number of paper clips? _____
- Which magnet pulled the paper clip the longest distance? _____
- Were they the same magnet? _____

How Strong Is It?

Name _____

Electromagnets are used in many places; they help run devices like motors and telephones. Here's your chance to make an electromagnet and test its strength.

1. Build an electromagnet according to your teacher's directions.
2. Unbend a paper clip until it looks like this: ⊂‗⊃. Place the clip on the tip of the magnet.
3. Hang one small paper clip at a time on the large clip. Do this until the large clip falls off the magnet. The strength of the magnet will be the number of paper clips the magnet held before the large clip fell off. Record the strength on the chart.
4. Repeat the test four more times. Use a different length of wire each time. Record your results.
5. Use the information to fill in the bar graph.

You will need:

An electromagnet
Forty paper clips
One large paper clip
Four lengths of wire
Pencil

| | **Wire length** (in feet) | | | | |
	2	3	4	5	6
Strength (in paper clips)					

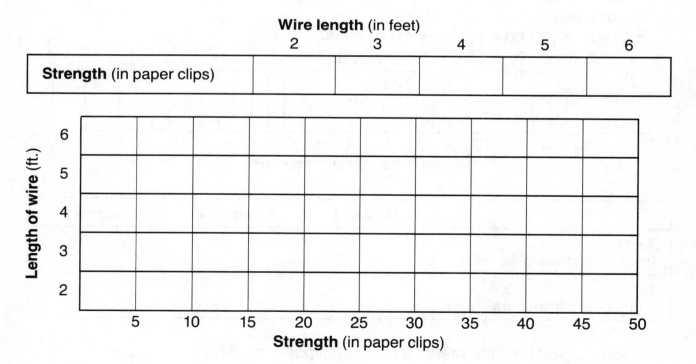

- How could you make an electromagnet stronger? _____

- How could you make an electromagnet weaker? _____

Adventures in Physical Science, © 1987 David S. Lake Publishers

What Type of Circuit?

There are two different types of circuits, *series* circuits and *parallel* circuits. In a series circuit, all the parts of the circuit are connected one after the other. The current can follow only one path. In a parallel circuit, the parts are connected in different ways. The current can follow more than one path. Look at the samples below. Then look at the circuits on the page. Decide if each circuit is a series circuit or a parallel circuit. Write *series* or *parallel* on the blank under the circuit.

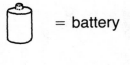 = battery

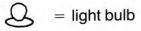 = light bulb

 = wire

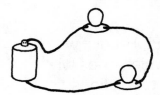

series

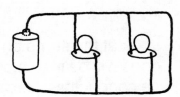

parallel

_____

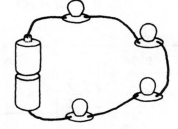

_____

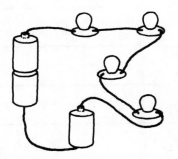

_____

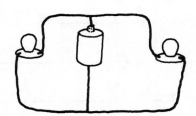

_____

_____

Conductors and Insulators

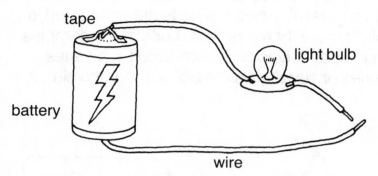

Name _____

1. Connect the wire, light bulb, and battery like this:

    tape

    battery

    light bulb

    wire

You will need:

A flashlight battery
Light bulb and socket
Insulated wire
Electrical tape
Aluminum foil
Door key
Paper cup
Nickel
Rubber band
Pencil
Wood or plastic ruler

2. Look at the items on the chart. Predict which ones will be insulators and which ones will be conductors. Record your predictions.
3. Hold the uncovered end of each wire to the aluminum foil. What happened to the light bulb?
4. On your chart, record whether aluminum is a conductor or an insulator.
5. Repeat steps 3 and 4 for each item.

Item Tested	Prediction	Conductor	Insulator
aluminum foil			
door key			
paper cup			
nickel			
rubber band			
pencil			
ruler			

- What do the items that were conductors have in common? _____
- What do the items that were insulators have in common? _____

Adventures in Physical Science, © 1987 David S. Lake Publishers

Seeing Your Voice

Name _____

1. Remove both ends of the coffee can or the oatmeal container. Cut a piece of the balloon large enough to be stretched tightly over one end of the container. Secure the balloon with a rubber band.
2. Glue the mirror onto the balloon, slightly off center.
3. Hold the open end of the container up to your mouth. Position the mirror so that a spot of sun (or a flashlight beam) reflects from the mirror onto a surface.
4. Hum a low-pitched note into the container. Observe the reflected spot of light. Try a high-pitched note, a soft speaking voice, and a loud speaking voice. Observe the light each time.

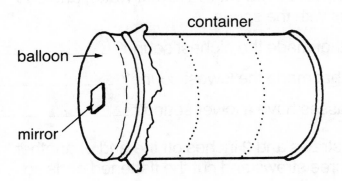

balloon

container

mirror

You will need:

A coffee can or an oatmeal container
Can opener
Scissors
Large balloon
Small mirror (1–2 cm)
Rubber band
Glue

- What happened to the spot when you talked or hummed?

_____

- Why do you think this happened?

_____

- What happened to the spot when you talked loudly?

_____

- What happened to the spot when you talked quietly?

_____

- What happened to the spot when you hummed a high-pitched sound?

_____

- What happened to the spot when you hummed a low-pitched sound?

_____

Playing with Pitch

Name _____

You will need:

Three glasses

Water

Measuring cup

Three paper straws

Scissors

Three thicknesses
of rubber bands

Shoe box

Spoon

1. Fill one of the glasses with ¼ cup of water, one with ⅓ cup of water, and one with ½ cup of water. Tap each glass with the spoon.

   How much water was in the glass that made the highest sound? _____

   How much water was in the glass that made the lowest sound? _____

   How could you make one of the glasses have a lower sound? _____

2. Cut 1 inch off the end of one of the straws and 2 inches off the end of another straw. Then flatten the ends of all three straws and cut the flattened ends so they look like this:

   Place the flattened end of the longest straw between your lips and blow. Repeat with the other two straws.

   Which straw made the highest sound? _____

   Which straw made the lowest sound? _____

   Would you hear a higher or lower sound if you cut off 3 inches from one of the

   straws? _____

3. Put the rubber bands around the open shoe box. Pluck each band.

   Which rubber band made the highest sound? _____

   Which rubber band made the lowest sound? _____

   What would happen if you changed the thickness of the rubber bands?

   _____

   What would happen if you changed the length of the rubber bands?

   _____

Adventures in Physical Science, © 1987 David S. Lake Publishers

Sequencing Sounds

Look at each row of pictures. Put the pictures in order by numbering each picture. Number the object that makes the lowest sound 1 and the object that makes the highest sound 4.

Bottles filled with water.

Flutes of different sizes.

Rubber bands of different thicknesses.

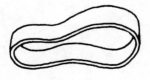 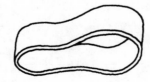  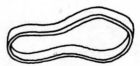

Adventures in Physical Science, © 1987 David S. Lake Publishers

Making Music

Look at the pictures. Decide whether each instrument is a wind instrument, a string instrument, or a percussion instrument. Write the name of the instrument in the column that tells what it is.

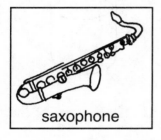
drum

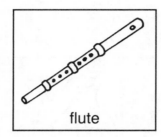
flute

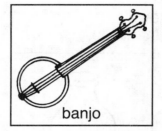
banjo

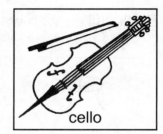
cello

saxophone

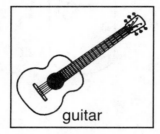
guitar

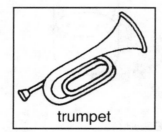
trumpet

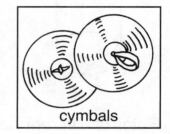
cymbals

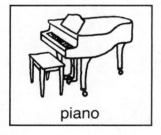
piano

xylophone

violin

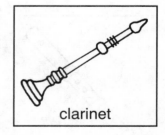
clarinet

Wind Instruments	String Instruments	Percussion Instruments
_____	_____	_____
_____	_____	_____
_____	_____	_____
_____	_____	_____
_____	_____	_____

- Which instrument has bars that vibrate? _____

- Which instruments have tubes in which air vibrates? _____

- Which instrument has six strings that vibrate? _____

Adventures in Physical Science, © 1987 David S. Lake Publishers

Turning Up the Volume

Name _____

Scientists can measure the loudness of a sound using a sound-level meter. A sound with a loudness of 0 decibels is a sound that most people can barely hear. A sound with a loudness of 210 decibels is so loud that it can make holes in certain materials. Use the following information to fill in the bar graph below.

- The sound of a jet plane has a strength of 135 decibels.
- The sound of a school cafeteria at lunchtime has a strength of 75 decibels.
- The sound of a vacuum cleaner has the strength of 60 decibels.
- The sound of a soft whisper has the strength of 20 decibels.
- The sound of a speaking voice has the strength of 40 decibels.
- The sound of a car horn has the strength of 110 decibels.

Jet plane														
Car horn														
Cafeteria														
Vacuum cleaner														
Speaking voice														
Whisper														

0 10 20 30 40 50 60 70 80 90 100 110 120 130 140

- If the sound of a rocket has the strength of 140 decibels, is it louder or softer than a jet plane? _____

- If the sound of thunder is 20 decibels less than that of a jet plane, how strong is the sound of thunder? _____

- The sound of rustling leaves has the strength of 5 decibels. Are rustling leaves louder or softer than a soft whisper? _____

Upon Reflection . . .

Look at each object on the page. Decide if the object reflects an image. If it does, write *image* under the object. If it doesn't, write *no image* under the object.

_____

_____

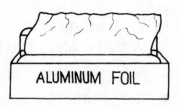

_____

_____

_____

_____

_____

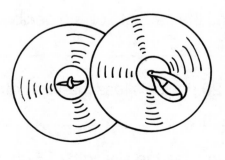

_____

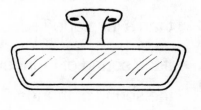

_____

Looking Through Lenses

Name _____

Your teacher will give you three types of lenses.

One will look like this: 〔 It is called a *flat* lens.

One will look like this: 〕 or ⧖ It is called a *concave* lens.

One will look like this: 〘 or 〇 It is called a *convex* lens.

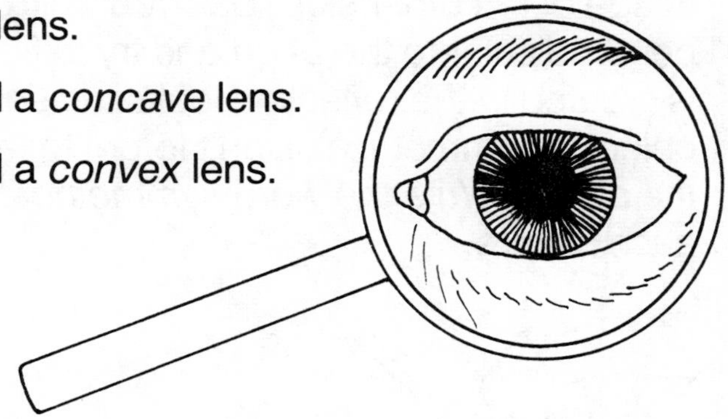

Look at five objects through each lens. Is the image of the object larger, smaller, or the same size as the object? Write down the results in the chart below.

	Flat Lens Larger, smaller, or same size?	**Concave Lens** Larger, smaller, or same size?	**Convex Lens** Larger, smaller, or same size?
Object 1			
Object 2			
Object 3			
Object 4			
Object 5			

● What happens to the image of an object when you look at it through a flat lens?

_____

● What happens to the image of an object when you look at it through a concave lens? _____

● What happens to the image of an object when you look at it through a convex lens? _____

Name _____

One way to describe something symmetrical is to say that one side is a mirror image of the other side. Use your mirror to test the objects below. Put the mirror perpendicular to the page and try to find an axis of symmetry. If the design that is created in the reflection looks the same as the real design on the page, the object is symmetrical. Don't forget to test for symmetry along different parts of the object. Write the word *symmetrical* or *asymmetrical* (not symmetrical) below each picture.

 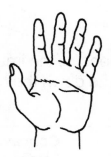 

_____ _____ _____

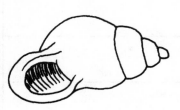 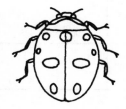 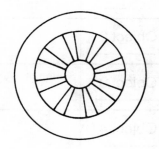

_____ _____ _____

A   C   8   5

_____ _____ _____ _____

Adventures in Physical Science, © 1987 David S. Lake Publishers

Red + Blue + Green = ?

Name _____

What happens if you mix red, blue, and green? Try this experiment and find out!

1. Color the circles on page 42 according to the directions. Cut out the circles and glue them on the cardboard. When the glue is dry, cut out the cardboard circles.
2. Use your pencil or a nail to punch out the two holes in each circle. Push a piece of string through each pair of holes. Knot the ends together. Your spinners should look like this:

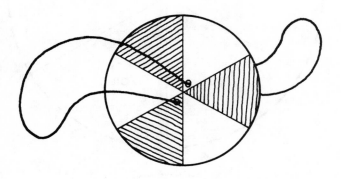

You will need:

8½″ × 11″ piece of cardboard

White glue

Red, blue, and green markers or crayons

Four pieces of two-foot-long string

Sharp pencil or nail

Scissors

3. Guess what color you will see when you spin each spinner. Record your guess on the chart.
4. Spin each spinner by holding the ends of the string and flipping the spinner to twist the string. Pull the string in and out until the spinner spins quickly.
5. Look at the color or colors each spinner makes. Write the results in the chart.

	red + blue	red + green	blue + green	red + blue + green
Guess				
Actual				

Name _____

Use these circles with page 41.
Color the circles as indicated.
Cut out the circles.

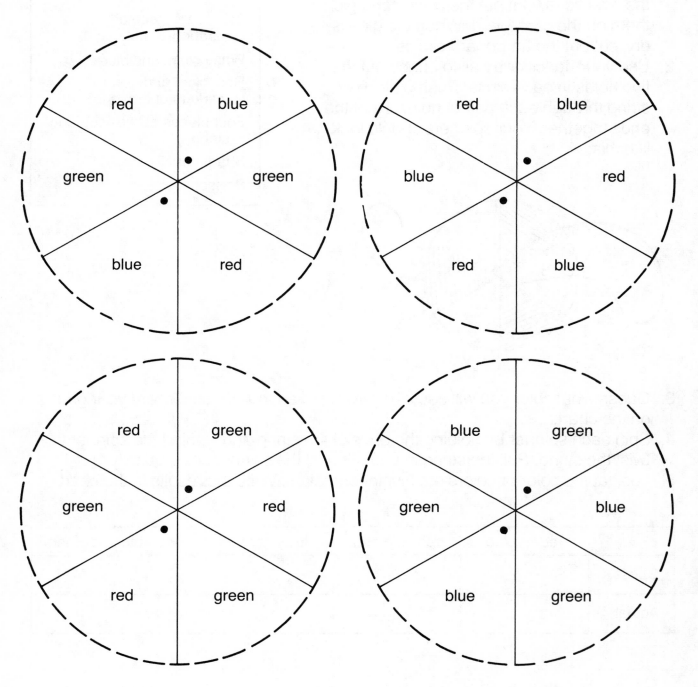

Disappearing Colors

What happens when you mix red light and blue paper? Or green light and red paper? Try this and find out!

1. Draw and cut out four 3″ construction-paper circles—one red, one blue, one green, and one white.
2. Place the circles on a desk. Turn on the flashlight and darken the room. Observe and record the colors that the circles seem to be.
3. Cover the flashlight with several layers of red cellophane. Fasten with a rubber band. Shine the flashlight on the circles. Observe and record the colors you see.
4. Repeat step 3 using blue cellophane instead of red cellophane.
5. Repeat step 3 using green cellophane instead of blue cellophane.

You will need:

Flashlight

Red, green, and blue cellophane

Red, green, blue, and white construction paper

Scissors

Rubber band

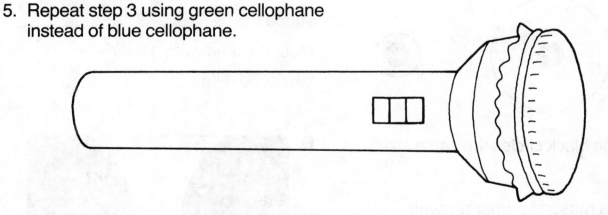

	white paper	red paper	blue paper	green paper
white light				
red light				
blue light				
green light				

Name _____

If you see something, is it real? Here are a few ways to test whether your eyes always tell you the truth or if they sometimes deceive you.

A.
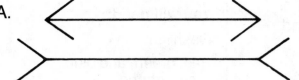

Are these two lines the same

length? _____

Measure them with a ruler.

Were you right? _____

B.
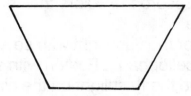

Is the top line of the first shape longer

than the top line of the second

shape? _____

Measure them with a ruler.

Were you right? _____

C.
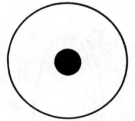

Are the black circles the same size?

_____

Give a reason for your answer.

_____

_____

_____

_____

_____

D.

How many different objects do you see

in this picture? _____

What are they? _____

_____

Adventures in Physical Science, © 1987 David S. Lake Publishers